OUTDOOR &
GARDEN PROJECTS

Albert Jackson and David Day

Hearst Books
A Division of Sterling Publishing Co., Inc.
New York

Popular Mechanics
Steve Willson, U.S. Project Editor
Tom Klenck, U.S. Art Director

Created, edited, and designed by Inklink
Concept, editorial, design and art direction: Simon Jennings
Text: Albert Jackson and David Day
Design: Alan Marshall
Illustrations: David Day, Robin Harris, Brian Craker,
    Michael Parr, Brian Sayers
Photographs: Paul Chave, Peter Higgins, Simon Jennings,
    Albert Jackson

Hearst Books
Project editor: Joseph Gonzalez
Cover design: Celia Fuller

Library of Congress Cataloging-in-Publication Data available.

10 9 8 7 6 5 4 3 2 1

Published by Hearst Books
A Division of Sterling Publishing Co., Inc.
387 Park Avenue South, New York, NY 10016

Popular Mechanics and Hearst Books are registered trademarks of Hearst Communications, Inc.

www.popularmechanics.com

For information about custom editions, special sales, premium and corporate purchases, please contact Sterling Special Sales Department at 800-805-5489 or specialsales@sterlingpub.com.

Distributed in Canada by Sterling Publishing
c/o Canadian Manda Group, 165 Dufferin Street
Toronto, Ontario, Canada M6K 3H6

ISBN-13: 978-1-58816-532-9
ISBN-10: 1-58816-532-9

Contents

Planning a garden

Consider the details
(above and bottom)
Period cast ornaments that add character to a garden need not cost a fortune.

Juxtaposing textures
Create eye-catching focal points, using well-considered combinations of natural form and texture.

Designing a garden is not an exact science. You may, for example, find that plants don't thrive in a particular spot, even though you have selected species that are recommended for your soil conditions and for the amount of sunlight your garden receives. And trees don't always conform to the size specified in a catalog. Nevertheless, forward planning can help avoid some of the more unfortunate mistakes, such as laying a patio where it will be in shade for most of the day, or digging a fishpond that's too small to create the conditions required for fish. Concentrate on planning the more permanent features first, taking into consideration how they will affect the planted areas of the garden that are to follow.

Deciding on the approach
Before you put pencil to paper, think about the type of garden you want, and ask yourself whether it will sit happily with your house and its immediate surroundings. Is it to be a formal garden, laid out in straight lines and geometric patterns—a style that often marries successfully with modern houses? Or do you prefer the more relaxed style of a rambling cottage garden? If you opt for the latter, remember that natural informality may not be as easy to achieve as you think, and your planting scheme will probably take several years to mature into the romantic garden you have in mind. Or maybe you're attracted to the idea of a Japanese-style garden—in effect a blend of both these styles, with every plant, stone, and pool of water carefully positioned, so that the garden bears all the hallmarks of a man-made landscape and yet conveys a sense of natural harmony.

Getting inspired
There's no shortage of material from which you can draw inspiration—there are countless books and magazines devoted to garden planning and design. Since no two gardens are completely alike, you probably won't find a plan that fits your plot exactly, but you may be able to adapt a design to suit your needs, or integrate some eye-catching details into your scheme.

Visiting real gardens is an even better way of getting inspired. Although large country estates and city parks are designed on a grand scale, you will be able to glean from them how mature shrubs should look or how plants, stone, and water can be used in a rock or water garden.

Don't forget that your friends may have had to tackle problems similar to your own—and if nothing else, you may learn from their mistakes!

Planning on a small scale
Good garden design does not rely on having a large plot of land. Here, curved shapes draw the eye through a delightful array of foliage and flowers planted around a beautifully manicured lawn and a small but perfectly balanced fishpond.

Surveying the plot

To make the best use of your plot of land, you need to take fairly accurate measurements and check prevailing conditions.

Measuring up
Make a note of the overall dimensions of your plot. At the same time, check the diagonal measurements, as your garden may not be a perfect rectangle or square. Diagonals are especially important when plotting irregular shapes.

Slopes and gradients
Check how the ground slopes. Jot down the direction of the slope and plot the points where the gradient begins and ends. You can get some idea of the differences in level by using a long straightedge and a level. Place one end of the straightedge on the top of a bank, for example, and measure the vertical distance from the other end to the foot of the slope.

Keep any useful features
Plot the position of existing features, such as paths and trees.

How about the weather?
Check the sun's passage and the direction of prevailing winds. Don't forget that the sun's angle of will be higher in summer.

Soil conditions
The type of soil in your garden will influence your choice of plants, but you can easily adjust soil content by adding peat or fertilizers. Clay soil is heavy when wet and tends to crack when dry. Sandy soil feels gritty and loose in dry conditions. Acidic peat soil is dark brown and flaky. Pale, chalky soil will not support acid-loving plants. Soil with too many stones or gravel is unsuitable as topsoil.

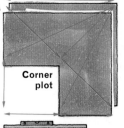

Measuring a plot
To draw an accurate plan, take down the overall dimensions, including the diagonals.

Irregular plot

Corner plot

Sloping site

Gauging a slope
Use a straightedge and a level to measure the height of a bank.

Theme gardens
Deciding on a style or theme for your garden will help you with the overall planning right from the start. The very different themes shown here include the seemingly random planting of a colorful cottage garden, the pleasing symmetry of a formal layout, and the "natural" informality of a Japanese-style garden that, in reality, is constructed with care from selected rocks, pebbles, and sculptural foliage.

Planning in greater detail

Juxtaposing textures
Create eye-catching focal points using well-considered combinations of natural form and texture.

Armed with all the measurements you've taken, make a simple drawing to try out your ideas. Then, to make sure that your plan will work in reality, mark out the shapes and plot the important features in your garden.

Drawing a plan
Draw a plan of your garden on paper. It must be a properly scaled plan or you are sure to make some errors, but it need not be professionally perfect. Use graph paper to plot the dimensions, but do the actual drawing on tracing paper laid over the grid so you can try out several ideas and adapt your plan without having to redraw it each time.

Plotting your design on the ground
Planning on paper is only the first stage. Gardens are rarely seen from above, so it is essential to plot the design on the ground to check your dimensions and view the features from different angles.

A pond or patio that seems enormous on paper may look pathetically small in reality. Other shortcomings, such as the way a tree will block the view from your proposed patio, become obvious once you lay out the plan full size.

Plot individual features by driving pegs into the ground and stretching string lines between them.

Use a rope tied to a peg to scribe arcs on the ground and mark the curved lines with stakes or a row of bricks. A garden hose provides the ideal aid for marking out less regular curves. If you can scrape areas clear of weeds, that will define the shapes still further.

Practical experiments
When you have marked out your design, carry out a few experiments to check that it is practicable.

Will it be possible, for instance, for two people to pass each other on the garden path without having to step into the flowerbeds? Can you set down a wheelbarrow on the path without one of its legs slipping into the pond?

Try placing some furniture on the area you have marked out for your patio to make sure there is enough room to relax comfortably and sit down to a meal with visitors. Most people build a patio alongside the house, but if you have to put it elsewhere to find a sunny spot, will it become a chore to walk back and forth with drinks and snacks?

Siting a pond
Position a pond to avoid overhanging trees and in an area where it will catch at least half a day's sunlight. Check that you can reach it with a hose and that you can run electrical cables to power a pump or lighting.

Commonsense safety
Don't make your garden an obstacle course. A narrow path alongside a pond, for example, may be hazardous or intimidating for an elderly relative, and low walls or planters near the edge of a patio could cause someone to trip.

Driveways and parking spaces
Allow a minimum width of 10 feet for a driveway, making sure there is enough room to open the doors of a car parked alongside a wall. And bear in mind that vehicles larger than your own might need to use the drive or parking space. If possible, allow room for the turning circle of your car; make sure you will have a clear view of the traffic when you pull out into the road.

Don't neglect your neighbors
There are legal restrictions regarding what you can erect in your garden. However, even if you have a free license, it's worth consulting your neighbors in case anything you're planning might inconvenience them. A wall or row of trees that throws shade across a neighbor's patio or blocks the light to their windows could be the source of a bitter dispute that lasts for years.

Plotting curved features
Use rope tied to a peg to lay out circles and arcs on the ground.

Draw a garden plan on tracing paper

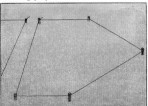
Mark out straight lines with pegs and string

Use rope tied to a peg to scribe an arc

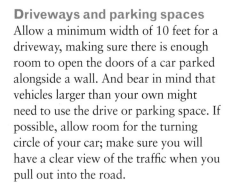
Try out irregular curves with a garden hose

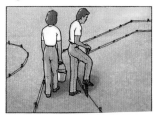
Make sure two people can pass on a path

There's a widely held belief that climbing plants, especially ivy, will damage any masonry wall. If exterior stucco or the mortar between bricks or stonework is in poor condition, then a vigorous ivy plant will undoubtedly weaken the structure as its aerial roots attempt to extract moisture from the masonry. The roots will invade broken joints and, on finding a source of nourishment for the main plant, expand and burst the weakened material. This encourages damp to penetrate the wall.

However, when clinging to sound masonry, ivy can do no more than climb using its suckerlike roots for support.

This growth can be controlled with the aid of training wires. As long as the structure is sound and free from damp, there is even some benefit in allowing a plant to clothe a wall, since its close-growing mat of leaves, mostly with their drip tips pointing downward, acts as insulation and provides some protection against the elements.

Climbers must be pruned regularly so they don't penetrate between the roofing or clog gutters and downspouts. If a robust climber is allowed to grow unchecked, the weight of the mature plant may eventually topple a weakened wall.

When planning your garden, you will probably want to include one or two trees. Think carefully, however, about your choice of trees and their position—they could potentially be damaging to the structure of your house if planted too near to it.

Siting trees

Tree roots searching for moisture can do considerable harm to a house's drainage system. Large roots can fracture rigid pipes and penetrate joints, eventually blocking drainage.

Before planting a tree close to the house, find out how far its root system is likely to spread. One solution is to estimate its likely maximum height and take this as a guide as to how far from the house you should plant the tree.

If you think an existing tree is likely to cause problems in the future, don't chop it down without consulting your local planning department—some trees are protected by preservation orders, and you could be fined if you cut down a protected tree without permission. Instead, hire a professional tree surgeon, who may be able to solve the problem by pruning the branches and roots.

Cracks: subsidence and heave

Minor cracks in foundation walls are often the result of shrinkage as the structure dries out. Such cracks are not serious and can be repaired during normal maintenance. More serious structural cracks, on the other hand, are due to movement of the foundations. Trees planted too close to a building can add to the problem by removing moisture from the site, causing subsidence of the foundations as the supporting earth collapses. Tree felling can be just as damaging; the surrounding soil, which has stabilized over the years, swells as it takes up the moisture that had previously been removed by the tree's root system. As a result, upward movement of the ground—known as heave—distorts the foundations, and cracks begin to appear.

Subsidence
A mature tree growing close to a house can draw so much water from the ground that the earth subsides, causing damage to the foundations.

Heave
When a mature tree is felled, the earth can absorb more water, causing it to swell until it displaces the foundations of the building.

Choosing fences

Log fencing
Construct your own informal fencing, using split logs nailed to horizontal rails.

Chain-link fencing

Trellis fencing

Post-and-chain fencing

A fence is the most popular form of boundary marker or garden screen, primarily because it is relatively inexpensive and takes very little time to erect, compared with building a wall.

Value for money

In the short term a fence is cheaper than a masonry wall, although one can argue that the cost of maintenance and replacement over a very long period eventually cancels out the savings. Wood has a comparatively short life because it is susceptible to insect infestation and rot when exposed to the elements. However, a fence can last for years if it is treated regularly with a preservative. And, if you're prepared to spend a little more money on plastic or concrete components, then your fence will be virtually maintenance free.

Selecting your fencing

You may be surprised by how much fencing you need to surround even a small garden. It's worth considering the available options carefully to make sure you invest your money in a fence that will meet your needs. Unless your priority is to keep neighborhood children or animals out of your garden, privacy is most likely to be the prime consideration. There are a number of privacy options, but you may have to compromise to some extent if you plan to erect a fence on a site exposed to strong prevailing winds. In this situation, you will need a fence that will act as a windbreak without offering so much resistance that the posts work loose within a couple of seasons.

Planning and planning permission

As a general rule, you can build a fence up to 6 feet high without having to obtain planning permission. However, if your boundary adjoins a highway, you may not be allowed to erect any barrier higher than 3 feet. In addition, there could be restrictions on fencing if the land surrounding your house has been designed as an open-plan area. Even so, many authorities will permit you to erect low boundary markers such as post-and-chain fencing.

Discuss your plans with your neighbors, because you will need their permission if you want to work from both sides of the boundary when erecting the fence. Check the exact line of the boundary to make certain that you don't encroach upon your neighbor's land. The fenceposts should run along the boundary or on your side of the line; before you dismantle an old fence, make sure that it is indeed yours to demolish.

If a neighbor is unwilling to replace an unsightly fence and won't even allow you to replace it at your expense, there is nothing to stop you from erecting another fence alongside the original one, provided that it's on your property.

Although it is an unwritten law that a good neighbor erects a fence with the post and rails facing his or her own property, there are usually no legal restrictions that could force you to do so.

Types of fencing

Chain-link fencing

Consisting of wire netting stretched between posts, chain-link fencing is purely functional. A true chain-link fence is made from strong galvanized or plastic-coated wire mesh that is suspended from a heavy-gauge cable, known as a straining wire, strung between the posts. You can make a cheap fence from soft wire netting or chicken wire, but it will not be durable and it will stretch if a large animal leans against it.

Decorative wire fencing, which is available at many garden centers, is designed primarily for marking boundaries or supporting lightweight climbing plants. Except in a remote rural location, any chain-link fence will benefit from a screen of climbers or hedging plants.

Types of fencing

Trellis fencing

An open trellis, constructed from thin softwood or from cedar lath, is designed primarily to help plants climb a wall, but rigid panels made from softwood battens can be used in conjunction with fenceposts to erect a substantial freestanding screen. Most garden centers stock a wide range of these decorative panels. A similar fence made from split rustic poles nailed to heavy rails and posts forms a strong and attractive barrier.

Post-and-chain fencing

A post-and-chain fence is no more than a decorative feature intended to prevent people from inadvertently wandering off a path or pavement onto a lawn or flowerbed. This type of fencing is constructed by stringing lengths of painted metal or plastic chain between short posts sunk into the ground.

Closedboard fencing

A closedboard fence is made by nailing overlapping strips (sometimes called featherboards) to horizontal rails. Featherboards are sawn planks that taper across their width, from 5/8 inch at the thicker edge down to about 1/8 inch. The boards are usually 4 or 6 inches wide. The best quality featherboards are made from cedar, but softwood is the usual choice in view of the amount of lumber required to make a long closedboard fence. Although it is expensive, closedboard fencing forms a screen that is both strong and attractive. Because the boards are attached vertically, the fence is quite difficult to climb from the outside—which makes it ideal for keeping intruders out.

Prefabricated panel fencing

Fences made from prefabricated panels nailed between posts are very popular, perhaps because they are so easy to erect. Standard fence panels are 6 feet wide and range in height from 2 to 6 feet. They are supplied in 1-foot gradations. Most fence panels are made from interwoven or overlapping strips of wood sandwiched between a frame of sawn lumber.

Overlapping-strip panels are usually designated as "lap" panels. When the strips have a natural wavy edge, they are sometimes called rustic lap.

Any panel fence tends to be a good value for the money and will provide reasonably durable screening, but if privacy is a consideration, choose the lapped type, as interwoven strips can shrink in the summer, leaving gaps in the fence.

Interlap fencing

An interlap fence is made by nailing square-edged boards to horizontal rails, fixing the boards alternately on one side, then the other. Spacing is a matter of choice. You can overlap the edges of the boards for privacy or space them apart to create a more decorative effect. This type of fencing is a sensible choice for a windy site. Although it's a sturdy screen, it permits a strong wind to pass through the gaps between the boards, reducing the amount of pressure exerted on the fence. Being equally attractive from either side, an interlap fence is perfect as boundary screening.

Picket fencing

The traditional low picket fence is still popular as a barrier at the front of the house, particularly where a high fence would look out of place. Narrow, vertical pickets with rounded or pointed tops are spaced at about 2 inches apart. Because they are time consuming to build by hand, some picket fences are sold as ready-made panels constructed from plastic or softwood to keep down the cost.

Ranch-style fencing

Low-level fences—made from simple horizontal rails fixed to short posts—are the modern counterpart of picket fencing. Used extensively to divide up building plots in some housing developments, ranch-style fencing is often painted, although clear-finished or stained lumber is just as attractive and much more durable. Softwood and some hardwoods are commonly used for this kind of fencing, but plastic ranch-style fences are also popular for their clean, crisp appearance. And, because there's no need to repaint them, very little maintenance is necessary.

Concrete fencing

A cast-concrete fence is maintenance free, and it provides the security and permanence of a wall built from brick or stone. Interlocking horizontal sections are built one upon the other, up to the required height. Each vertical stack is supported by grooves cast into the sides of concrete fenceposts. This relatively heavy fencing would be dangerous if the posts were not firmly embedded in concrete.

Closedboard fencing

Panel fencing

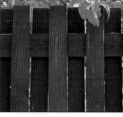
Interlap fencing

Picket fencing

Ranch-style fencing

Concrete fencing

Fenceposts

Whatever type of fence you decide to erect, its strength and durability will rely on good-quality posts set solidly in the ground. Erecting the posts carefully and accurately is crucial to the longevity of the fence and may save you having to either rebuild or repair it in the future.

Types of post

In some cases, the nature of the fencing will determine the choice of post. Concrete fencing, for example, has to be supported by compatible concrete posts. Generally, though, you can choose the material and style of post that suits the appearance of the fence.

Timber posts
Most fences are supported by square-section wood posts.Standard fencepost sizes are 3 or 4 inches square, but gate posts are often 5, 6, or 8 inches square. Unless you ask specifically for hardwood, most lumberyards supply pretreated softwood posts.

Plastic posts
Extruded PVC (polyvinyl chloride) posts are supplied with plastic fencing, together with molded-plastic end caps and other plastic components.

Concrete posts
A variety of reinforced-concrete posts, usually 4 inches square, are produced to suit different styles of fence—drilled for chain-link fixings, mortised for rails, and recessed or grooved for panels. Special corner and end posts are notched to accommodate bracing struts for chain-link fencing.

Metal posts
Steel posts are made to support chain-link fences, and wrought-iron gates are often hung from plastic-coated steel posts. Steel posts are very sturdy, but are not usually considered the most attractive option for residential use.

Capping fenceposts
If you simply cut the end of a wood post square, the top of the post will rot relatively quickly. The solution is to cut a single or double bevel to shed the rainwater, or nail a wooden or galvanized-metal cap over the end of the post.

Preserving fenceposts
Wood that is to be in contact with the ground benefits from prolonged immersion in a polyethelene-lined trough of chemical wood preserver. Even when a wood fencepost is pretreated to prevent rot, you can make doubly sure by soaking the base of each post in a bucket of chemical preserver overnight.

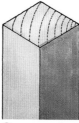 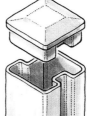
Square wood post | **Capped plastic post**

Drilled concrete post | **Mortised concrete post**

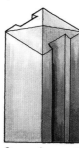 
Grooved concrete post | **Notched end post**

Angle-iron post | **Tubular-steel post**

Untreated timber posts quickly succumb to rot.

If you are replacing an old fence, it may prove convenient to put the new posts in the same position as the old. Begin by dismantling the boards and rails, or cut through the hardware so you can remove the fence panels. If any of the posts are bedded firmly or sunk into concrete, you will have to pry them out.

Start by removing the topsoil from around each post to loosen it. Drive large nails into two opposite faces of the post, about one foot from the ground. Bind a length of rope around the post, just below the nails, and tie the ends to the tip of a pry board. Build a pile of bricks or place a concrete block close to the post, and use it as a fulcrum to lever out the post.

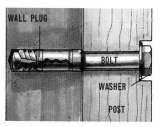

Removing a rotted fencepost
Use a pry board to lever a post out of the ground.

Fixing to a wall
If a fence runs up to the house, attach the first post to the wall, using three expanding masonry bolts. Place a washer under each bolt head to stop the wood from being crushed. Using a level, check that the post is vertical and, if need be, drive shims between the post and wall to make adjustments.

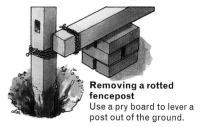

Bolting a post to a wall
If you are attaching a prefabricated panel against a wall-fixed post, counterbore the bolts so that the heads lie flush with the surface of the wood.

Using metal sockets

Fencepost spikes

Bolted sockets
Bolt this type of socket to existing patios and concrete drives.

Embedded sockets
Embed these sockets in wet concrete.

Repair socket
Allows replacement of rotten or broken posts set in concrete. Cut off the old post flush with the concrete and then drive the spike into the center of the stump.

Instead of digging holes for your fenceposts, you can place the base of each post into a square socket attached to a metal spike that is driven into firm ground. Similar sockets can be bolted to existing paving or set in fresh concrete.

Use 2-foot spikes for fences up to 4 feet high, and 30-inch spikes for a 6-foot fence. Place a scrap of hardwood post into the socket to protect the metal and then drive the spike partly into the ground with a sledgehammer.

Hold a level against the socket to make certain the spike is vertical **(1)**, then hammer the spike into the ground until only the socket is visible. Insert the post and, depending on the type of spike, secure it by screwing through the side of the socket or by tightening clamping bolts **(2)**. If you're putting up a panel fence, use the edge of a fixed panel to position the next spike **(3)**.

1 Use a level to check that spike is vertical

2 Fix the post

3 Position next spike

The type of fence you choose dictates whether you need to erect all the posts first or put them up one at a time, along with the other components. For a prefabricated panel fence, fix the posts as you erect the fence; for a chain-link fence, complete the run of posts first.

Marking out a row of fenceposts

Drive a peg into the ground at each end of the fence run, and stretch a length of string between the pegs to align the row of posts. If possible, adjust the spacing to avoid obstructions such as large tree roots. If one or more posts have to be inserted across a paved patio, either lift enough slabs to allow you to dig the required holes, or mark out the patio for bolt-down, metal post sockets (see left).

Erecting the posts

Bury one quarter of each post to provide a firm foundation. You can rent posthole augers to remove the central core of earth. Twist the tool to drive it into the ground **(1)** and pull it out after every 6 inches to remove the soil. When you have reached a sufficient depth, taper the sides of the hole slightly so that you can backfill easily around the post.

To anchor the post, start by packing a layer of small stones into the bottom of the hole to support the base of the post and provide drainage. Have someone hold the post upright while you brace it with boards nailed to the post and to stakes driven into the ground. Use guy ropes to support a concrete post. Check with a level that the post is vertical **(2)**.

Pack more soil around the post, leaving a hole about 1 foot deep for filling with concrete. Fill up with a fast-setting dry concrete mix made specially for erecting fence posts, then pour in the recommended amount of water. Or mix up general-purpose concrete and tamp it into the hole with the end of a board **(3)**. Form the concrete just above soil level so that it slopes away from the post. This will help shed rain-water.

Leave the concrete to harden before removing the braces. Support a panel fence temporarily, with braces wedged against the posts.

1 Dig the posthole

2 Check for level

3 Fill with concrete

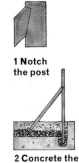

1 Notch the post

2 Concrete the end post

Supporting end posts

Chain-link fenceposts made of wood must resist the tension of the straining wires. Brace each end post (and some of the intermediate ones, over a long run) with a strut made from a length of fencepost. Shape the end of the strut to fit a notch cut into the post **(1)** and nail it in place.

Anchor the post in the ground in the usual way, but dig a trench about 18 inches deep alongside for the strut. Wedge a brick under the end of the strut before packing the soil around the post and strut. Fill the trench up to ground level with concrete **(2)**. Support a corner post with two struts set at right angles.

Putting up chain-link fencing

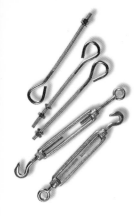

To support chain-link fencing, set out a row of posts, spaced no more than 10 feet apart. Brace end posts with struts to resist the straining wires' pull. Brace intermediate posts in a long run every 200 feet or so.

Using wood posts

Support chain-link fencing on straining wires (see right). Since it's impossible to tension this heavy-gauge wire by hand, large straining bolts are used to stretch it between the posts: one to coincide with the top of the fencing, one about 6 inches from the ground, and a third, if required, midway between.

Drill ⅜-inch-diameter holes right through the posts, insert a bolt into each hole, and fit a washer and nut (1), leaving enough thread to provide about 2 inches of movement once you begin to apply tension to the wire.

Pass the end of the wire through the bolt's eye, then twist it around itself with pliers (2). Stretch the wire along the run of fencing, stapling it to each post and strut (3), but leave enough slack for the wire to move when tensioned.

Cut the wire to length and twist it through the bolt at the other end of the fence. Tension the wire from both ends by turning the nuts with a wrench (4).

Standard straining bolts provide enough tension for the average garden fence, but over a long run of fencing—200 feet or more—use a turnbuckle for each wire (see left).

Using concrete posts

Fix straining wires to concrete posts, using a special bolt and cleat (see right). Bolt a stretcher bar to the cleats when erecting the wire netting. Secure the straining wires to intermediate posts by using a length of galvanized wire passed through each of the predrilled holes.

Using steel posts

Stretcher bars with winding brackets for applying tension to straining wires are supplied with steel fenceposts (see right).

Using a turnbuckle
Apply tension by turning the turnbuckle with an open-end wrench.

KNUCKLE
SPIRAL

Joining wire mesh
Chain-link fencing is usually supplied in 80-foot lengths. To join one roll to another, unfold the knuckles at each end of the first wire spiral, then turn the spiral counter-clockwise to withdraw it from the mesh. Connect the two rolls by rethreading the loose spiral in a clockwise direction through each link of the mesh. Bend the knuckle over at the top and bottom.

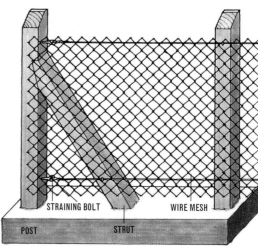
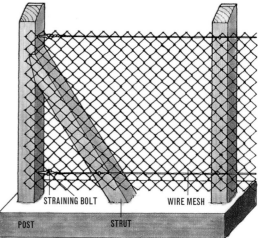

STRAINING BOLT   WIRE MESH
POST   STRUT

Chain-link fencing

Attaching the mesh
Staple each end link to the post. Unroll the mesh and pull it taut. Tie it to straining wires every 1 foot with galvanized wire. Attach to post at far end.

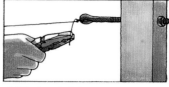

Staple mesh to post

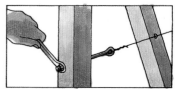

Tie with wire loops

1 Insert a straining bolt in end post   **2 Attach a straining wire to bolt**

3 Staple the wire to each post and strut   **4 Tension the bolt at the far end of fence**

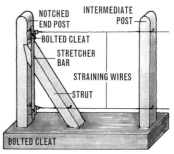

NOTCHED END POST   INTERMEDIATE POST
BOLTED CLEAT
STRETCHER BAR
STRAINING WIRES
STRUT
BOLTED CLEAT

Concrete fence posts

Cleat and stretcher bar   **Tie wire to post**

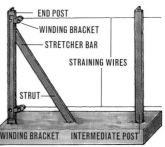

END POST
WINDING BRACKET
STRETCHER BAR
STRAINING WIRES
STRUT
WINDING BRACKET   INTERMEDIATE POST

Steel posts

Winding bracket   **Pass straining wire through predrilled hole in each intermediate post.**

Erecting closedboard fences

The boards used to panel a closedboard fence are nailed to triangular-section rails mortised into the fenceposts. Concrete posts, and some wooden ones, are supplied ready-mortised, but if you buy standard wood posts, you'll either have to cut the mortises yourself or use end brackets (see right) instead. Space fenceposts no more than 10 feet apart.

The ends of the fence boards are liable to rot, especially if they are in contact with the ground, so install horizontal boards at the foot of the fence. Nail capping strips across the tops of the boards.

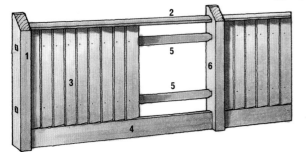

Closedboard fencing

Closedboard fencing
1 End post
2 Capping strip
3 Fence boards
4 Baseboard
5 Rail
6 Intermediate post

Capping the fence
Nail a wooden capping strip to the ends of the fence boards to shed rainwater.

Erecting the framework

When using plain wooden posts, mark and cut mortises for the rails about 6 inches above and below where the fence boards will be attached. For fencing over 4 feet high, cut mortises for a third rail midway between the others. Position the mortises 1 inch from the front face of each post.

As you erect the fence, cut the rails to length and shape a tenon on each end, using a coarse rasp or Surform file (1). Paint preservative onto the shaped ends and into the mortises before you assemble the rails.

Erect the first fencepost and pack soil around its base. Get someone to hold the post steady while you fit the rails and erect the next post, tapping it onto the ends of the

rails with a mallet (2). Check that the rails are horizontal and the posts vertical before packing soil around the second post. Construct the entire run of posts and rails in the same way. If you can't maneuver the last post onto the tenoned rails, cut the rails square and attach them to the post with metal end brackets.

Check the whole run once more to ensure that the rails are bedded firmly in their mortises and that the framework is true, then secure each rail by driving a nail through the post into the tenon (3) or by drilling a hole and inserting a wooden dowel. Pack concrete around each post and leave it to set.

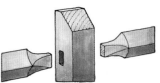

1 Shape rails to fit the mortises

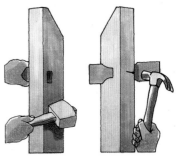

2 Tap post onto rails

3 Nail rails in place

Installing the boards

Baseboards Some concrete posts are mortised to take baseboards; in this case, fit the boards at the same time as the rails. If concrete posts are not mortised, bed treated wooden cleats into the concrete filling at the base of each post, and screw the baseboard to the cleat when the concrete has set.

To fit baseboards to wooden posts, nail cleats to the foot of each post, then nail the boards to the cleats (4). Some metal post sockets are made with brackets for attaching baseboards.

Fence boards Cut the fence boards to length and treat the endgrain with preservative. Stand the first fence board on the

baseboard, butting its thicker edge against the post. Nail the board to the rails with galvanized nails about ¾ inch from the thick edge. Place the next board in position, overlapping the thin edge of the fixed board by ½ inch. Check that it's vertical, then nail it in the same way. Don't drive a nail through both boards or they may split if the wood shrinks. To space the other boards equally, make a spacer block from a scrap of wood (5). Plane the last board to fit against the next post and attach it, this time with two nails per rail (6). Finally, nail capping strips across the tops of the fence boards, cut the posts to length, and cap them.

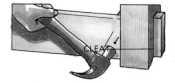

4 Nail baseboards to the cleats

5 Use a spacer block to position fence boards

6 Attach last board with two nails

Erecting panel fences

To prevent a fencing panel from rotting, either install baseboards, as on a closedboard fence, or leave a gap at the bottom by supporting a panel temporarily on two bricks while you attach it to the fenceposts.

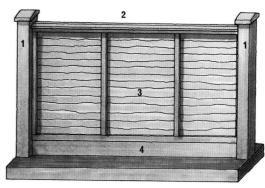

Panel fence
1 Fenceposts
2 Capping strip
3 Prefabricated panel
4 Baseboard

Using wood posts

Pack the first post into its hole with soil, then get someone to hold a panel against the post while you toenail through the frame into the post **(1)**. If you can work from both sides, drive three nails from each side of the fence. If the wood used for the frame is likely to split, blunt the nails by tapping their points with a hammer.

You can also use galvanized-metal angle brackets to secure the panels **(2)**. Construct the entire fence by erecting panels and posts alternately.

Install pressure-treated baseboards and nail capping strips across the panels if they have not already been installed by the manufacturer. Finally, cut each post to length and cap it.

Wedge struts made from scrap lumber against each post to keep it vertical, then top up the holes with concrete. If you're unable to work from both sides, you will have to fill each hole as you build the fence.

1 Nail the panel through its frame

2 Or use angle brackets to attach panels to posts

3 Concrete post grooved to take panels

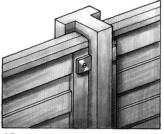

4 Recessed concrete post with hanging brackets

Using concrete posts

Grooved concrete posts will support panels without the need for additional hardware **(3)**. Recessed concrete posts are supplied with metal brackets for attaching the panels **(4)**.

Building a panel fence
Posts and panels are erected alternately. Dig a hole for the post **(1)** and hold it upright with packed soil. Support a panel on bricks **(2)** and get a helper to push it against the post **(3)** while you nail it **(4)**. Install baseboards **(5)** and capping strips **(6)**, then cap the posts **(7)**. Fill the holes with concrete **(8)** and allow it to set.

Erecting fences on sloping ground

Post-and-rail fences

Crossways slope
If a slope runs across your property so that a neighbor's yard is higher than your own, either build brick retaining walls between the posts or set paving slabs in concrete to hold back the soil.

Downhill slope
The posts need to be set vertically, even when you are erecting a fence on a sloping site. Chain-link fencing or ranch-style rails can follow the slope of the land if you wish; but fence panels should be stepped and the triangular gaps beneath them filled with baseboards or retaining walls.

Retaining wall for a crossways slope

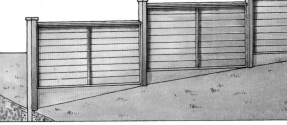
Step fence panels to allow for a downhill slope

Supporting a rotted post
Buried wood posts often rot below ground level, leaving a perfectly sound section above. To save an old post, you can make a passable repair by bracing the upper section with a short concrete post.

Erecting the post
First, dig the soil from around the rotted stump and remove it. Install a concrete post and pack soil around it **(1)**, then fill the hole with concrete **(2)**. Drill pilot holes in the wooden post for lagscrews **(3)**. Insert the screws, using a wrench to draw the old post tightly against the new one.

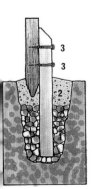

A simple ranch-style fence is no more than a series of horizontal rails attached to short posts concreted into the ground. A picket fence is similar but with vertical pickets attached to the rails.

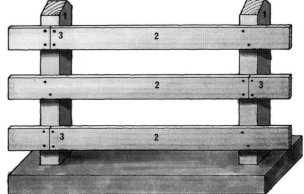

Ranch-style fence
1 Short posts
2 Horizontal rails
3 Rail joints

• Building plastic ranch-style fencing
The basic construction of a plastic fence is similar to one built from wood, but follow the manufacturer's instructions concerning the method for joining the rails to the posts.

Fixing horizontal rails
You can screw the rails directly to the posts **(1)**, but the fence is likely to last longer if you cut a shallow notch in the post to locate each rail before attaching it permanently in place **(2)**.

Join two horizontal rails by butting them over a fencepost **(3)**. Arrange to stagger such joints so that you don't end up with all the rails butted on the same posts **(4)**.

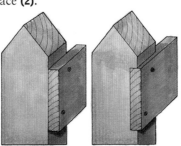 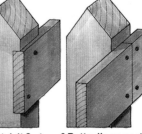 

1 Screw rail to post **2 Or notch it first** **3 Butt rails on posts** **4 Stagger rail joints**

Installing picket panels
When constructing a low picket fence from manufactured panels, which are designed to fit between the posts, it is best to buy or make steel saddle brackets for attaching a pair of panels to each post. Be sure to prime and paint homemade brackets to keep the steel from rusting.

Use a metal bracket to attach picket-fence panels

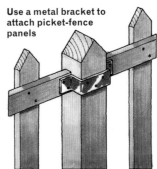

Choosing a gate

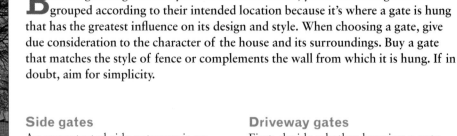

Browsing through lumberyards and home centers, you'll find that gates are grouped according to their intended location because it's where a gate is hung that has the greatest influence on its design and style. When choosing a gate, give due consideration to the character of the house and its surroundings. Buy a gate that matches the style of fence or complements the wall from which it is hung. If in doubt, aim for simplicity.

Gate styles

Side gates

Entrance gates

Driveway gates

Materials for gates
Many wood gates are made from relatively cheap softwood, but cedar or oak will last longer. Many so-called wrought-iron gates are actually made from mild-steel bar, which must be primed and painted to prevent rust.

Side gates
An unprotected side entrance is an open invitation for intruders to slip in unnoticed and gain access to the back of your house. Side gates are designed to deter burglars while affording easy access for visitors. These gates are usually between 6 and 7 feet high and are made from either wrought iron or wood. Wood gates are heavy and are therefore braced with strong diagonal members to keep them rigid. With security in mind, choose a closedboard or tongue-and-grooved gate because their vertical boards are difficult to climb. Attach strong hinges to the top and bottom.

Entrance gates
An entrance gate is designed as much for its appearance as its function, but it must be sturdy enough to withstand frequent use. For this reason, wood gates are often braced with a diagonal strut running from the top of the latch stile down to the bottom of the hinge stile. Don't hang a gate with the strut running the other way or the bracing will not work as well.

Common fence styles are reflected in the type of entrance gates you can buy. Picket, closedboard, and ranch-style gates are all available, and there are simple frame-and-panel gates made with solid wood or exterior-grade plywood panels that serve to keep the frame rigid. If the tops of both the stiles are cut at an angle, they will tend to shed rainwater, reducing the likelihood of wet rot.

Decorative iron gates are often used for entrances, but make sure the style is appropriate for the building and its location. A large, ornate gate can look out of place in front of a simple modern house.

Driveway gates
First, decide whether hanging a gate across your driveway is a good idea. Stepping out of your car in order to open the gate can be a problem unless there's plenty of room to pull the car off the road.

Driveway gates invariably open into the property, so if the drive slopes up from the road, make sure there's adequate ground clearance for a wide gate. You can also hang two smaller gates that meet in the center.

Gateposts and piers
Gateposts and masonry piers need to be anchored securely to the ground in order to take the leverage exerted by a heavy gate.

Choose hardwood posts whenever possible, and select the size according to the weight of the gate. Posts that are 4 inches square are adequate for entrance gates, but use 5-inch posts for gates that are 6 feet high. For a gate across a drive, choose posts that are 6 or even 8 inches square.

If you opt for concrete gateposts, look for posts predrilled to accept hinges and a catch. Otherwise, you may have to screw these fittings to a strip of wood bolted to the post.

Square or cylindrical tubular-steel posts are available with hinge pins, gate-stops, and catches welded in place. Unless they have been coated with plastic at the factory, steel posts must be painted to protect them from rust.

A pair of masonry piers is another possibility. Each pier should be at least 16 inches square and built on a firm concrete footing. For heavy gates, the hinge pier should be reinforced with rebar buried in the footing and running up through the pier.

Gateposts are set in concrete like ordinary fenceposts, but the postholes are linked by a concrete bridge that provides extra support.

Start by laying the gate on the ground with a post on each side. Check that the posts are parallel and that they are the required distance apart to accommodate hinges and catch. Nail two boards from post to post and another diagonally to keep the posts in line while you erect them **(1)**.

Dig a trench 1 foot wide across the entrance, making it long enough to accommodate both posts. It need be no deeper than 1 foot in the center, but dig an adequate posthole at each end—about 18 inches deep for a low entrance gate or 2 feet deep for a taller side gate.

Set the braced gateposts in the holes with soil and concrete, using temporary braces to hold them upright until the concrete has set **(2)**. Fill the trench with concrete and either level it flush with the surrounding ground or allow for the thickness of some paving.

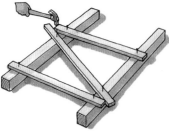

1 Nail temporary braces to gateposts

2 Support the posts until concrete sets

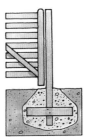

Supporting driveway gates
Hang wide, farm-style gates on posts set in holes 3 feet deep. Erect the latch post in concrete like any fencepost, but bolt a heavy piece of wood across the base of the hinge post before anchoring it in concrete.

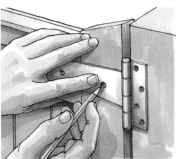

Mark positions of the hinges and catch

Hanging a gate
Stand the gate between the posts and prop it up on a pair of bricks or wood blocks to hold it the required height off the ground. Tap in pairs of wedges on each side of the gate until it is held securely. Then mark the positions of the hinges and catch.

A range of specialized hardware has been developed for hanging heavy garden gates to cope with the strain involved.

Hinges

Strap hinges Most side and entrance gates are hung on strap hinges. Screw the longer flap to the gate rail, and the vertical flap to the face of the post. Heavy gates require a hinge that's bolted through the top rail. Wide driveway gates are hung from double strap hinges made with long flaps bolted on each side of the top rail.

Hinge pins Collars, welded to metal gates, drop over hinge pins that are attached to the gateposts. To prevent a gate from being lifted off, drill a hole through the top pin and install a split pin and washer.

Latches and catches

Automatic latches Simple wood gates are usually outfitted with a latch that works automatically as the gate is closed.

Thumb latches Pass the lifter bar of a thumb latch through a slot cut in the gate, then screw the handle to the front. Attach the latch beam to the inner face so the lifter bar can raise the beam from the hooked keeper fixed to the gatepost.

Ring latches A ring latch works like a thumb latch but is usually operated from inside only by twisting the ring handle to lift the latch beam.

Chelsea catches Pivoting on a bolt that passes through the stile of a driveway gate, a Chelsea catch drops into a slot in the catch plate, which is screwed to the gatepost.

Loop-over catches When hanging a pair of wide gates, one is fixed with a bolt that slides into a socket buried into the ground. A U-shaped metal catch on the other gate drops over the stile of the fixed gate.

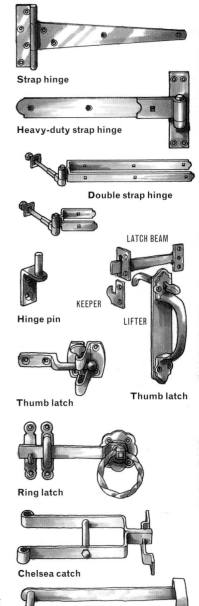

Strap hinge

Heavy-duty strap hinge

Double strap hinge

LATCH BEAM

KEEPER

Hinge pin

LIFTER

Thumb latch

Thumb latch

Ring latch

Chelsea catch

Chelsea catch

Masonry: building walls

Whatever kind of masonry structure you are building, the basic techniques are broadly similar. However, it's well worth hiring a professional builder or mason when the structure is complicated or extensive, especially if it will have to bear considerable loads or stress.

Amateur masons

It's difficult to suggest which aspects of bricklaying are likely to overstretch the capabilities of a do-it-yourselfer, as this differs from one individual to another and depends on the nature of the job. Clearly, it would be foolish for anyone to try to build a two-story house without having had a lot of experience or professional training. And even building a high boundary wall, which is simple in terms of technique, may be too difficult if the wall is very long or moves down, up, or across a sloping yard.

The simple answer is to practice with relatively low retaining walls, screens, and dividing walls until you have mastered the skills of laying bricks and blocks solidly one upon another and have developed the ability to build a wall that is straight and absolutely plumb.

Walls for different locations

Retaining walls

A retaining wall is designed to hold back a bank of earth when terracing a sloping site. Raised planting beds often serve a similar purpose.

Provided it's not excessively high, a retaining wall is quite easy to build, although, strictly speaking, it should slope back into the bank to resist the weight of the earth. You must also allow for drainage in order to reduce water pressure behind the wall.

Retaining walls can be constructed with bricks, concrete blocks, or stone. Sometimes they are piled up, but in many cases traditional mortar is used for the joints.

Boundary walls

A brick or stone wall that surrounds your property provides security and privacy while creating an attractive background for trees and shrubs.

New bricks complement a formal garden or a modern setting, while secondhand materials or undressed stone blend well with an old, established garden. If you aren't able to match existing masonry exactly, disguise the difference in color by brushing liquid fertilizer onto the wall to encourage lichen to grow. You can also hide the junction with a climbing plant.

You usually need a building permit to build a wall higher than 3 feet if it's near a highway, or over 6 feet high elsewhere.

Dividing walls

Many people like to divide up a yard with walls in order to add interest to an otherwise featureless site. For example, you can build a wall to form a visual break between a patio and an area of grass, or perhaps to define the edge of a pathway. This type of dividing wall is often no more than 2 feet high.

Your material options are many, but concrete blocks with textured surfaces and standard bricks are very popular.

Screen walls

Screens are dividing walls that provide a degree of privacy without completely masking the property beyond. They are usually built with decorative pierced blocks, sometimes combined with brick or solid-block bases and piers.

Stone retaining wall

Decorative concrete-block screen

Boundary wall of yellow brick

Cast concrete blocks make attractive dividing walls

Types of brick

Solid bricks

The majority of bricks are solid throughout, either flat on all surfaces or with a depression known as a "frog" on one face. When filled with mortar, the frog keys the bricks.

Cored or perforated bricks

Cored bricks have holes through them, performing the same function as the frog. A wall made with cored bricks must be covered on top with a course of solid bricks.

Special shapes

Specially shaped bricks are made for decorative brickwork. Masons draw upon the full range when building structures such as arches and chamfered or rounded corners.

Seconds
Seconds are secondhand, rather than second-rate, bricks. They should be cheaper than new bricks, but demand can inflate prices. Using seconds might be the only way you can match the color of weathered brickwork.

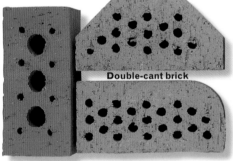

Standard cored brick   **Double-cant brick**   **Bullnose brick**

Standard brick with frog   **Cut brick for shaped corner**   **Half-round brick**

● **Storing bricks**
When bricks are delivered, have them unloaded as near as possible to the building site and stack them carefully on a flat, dry base. Cover the stack with a tarp until you're ready to use the bricks to prevent them from becoming saturated with rain.

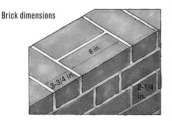

Brick dimensions

Choosing Bricks

Thousands of different types of bricks are produced in this country and around the world. Generally, your choice will be limited to bricks manufactured in your local area, because long-distance hauling of these heavy materials is too expensive for most applications. When buying brick, it's important to understand the basic classifications as they relate to size, appearance, and weathering characteristics.

Varieties of brick

Face brick Weather- and frost-resistant, face bricks are suitable for any type of exposed brickwork. Made as much for their appearance as for their structural qualities, face bricks come in the widest range of colors and textures. Face bricks are graded carefully to meet standards of strength, water absorption, and uniformity of shape.

Building brick Cheap general-purpose bricks, building bricks are used mainly for interior brickwork that will be plastered or stuccoed over. They are not color matched carefully, but the mottled effect of an exposed wall built with building bricks can be attractive. Although they can be damaged or cracked by frost if used in structural applications in exposed exterior locations, building bricks can be used for freestanding garden walls.

Firebrick Pale yellow in color, firebricks are made from specially chosen clays that are carefully fired to provide a highly heat-resistant product. They are designed for lining fireplaces, kilns, and barbecues. They must be laid up with heat-resistant mortar.

Durability of bricks

Building brick is manufactured in three grades that have different weathering characteristics and indicate the conditions a particular kind of brick is best suited to. For any particular project, check which kind of brick is required by your local building department.

Type SW (severe weathering) bricks are best suited for outdoor projects in areas prone to prolonged periods of freezing. Always choose type SW brick for patios and driveways. While there is a separate classification for bricks known as paving bricks, these are meant for public, high-traffic areas and are not required for residential projects.

Type MW (moderate weathering) can be used outdoors in areas where there is little or no frost. In most cases type MW bricks can be used for constructing garden walls, even in cold regions.

Type NW (no weathering) bricks are meant only for indoor use, but they can be used occasionally for outdoor structures that will be protected by an overhang from the ravages of driven rain and snow.

Buying bricks

Bricks are normally sold by the thousand, but most retailers are usually willing to sell smaller quantities. It is cheaper to order bricks from the producer, but only if you buy a load large enough to make shipping economical.

Estimating quantities The size of a standard brick is $2\frac{1}{4}$ x $3\frac{3}{4}$ x 8 inches. But because dimensions may vary by a fraction of an inch, even within the same batch of bricks, manufacturers normally specify a nominal size which includes an additional $\frac{1}{4}$ to $\frac{1}{2}$ inch to each dimension to allow for the mortar joint. To calculate how many bricks you need, allow about 48 bricks for every square yard of a wall. Add 5 percent for cutting and breakage.

Brick color and texture

The popularity of brick as a building material stems largely from its range of subtle colors and textures, which actually improve with weathering. Weathered brick can be difficult to match by using a manufacturer's catalog, so try to borrow samples from your supplier's stock—or, if you have spare bricks, take one to the supplier to compare it with new bricks.

Color

The color of bricks is largely determined by the type of clay used in their manufacture, although the color is modified by the addition of certain minerals and by the temperature of the firing. Large manufacturers supply a wide variety of colors, and you can also buy brindled (multicolored or mottled) bricks, which are useful for blending with existing masonry.

Texture

Texture is as important to the appearance of a brick wall as color. Simple rough or smooth textures are created by the choice of materials. Others are imposed upon the clay by scratching, rolling, brushing, and so on. A brick may be textured all over or on the sides and ends only.

Brick colors and textures
A small selection from the wide range of colors and textures.
1 Smooth blended
2 Handmade
3 Sand-faced yellow
4 Smooth blue engineering
5 Sand-faced gray
6 Smooth red stock
7 Wire-cut brindle
8 Textured multibuff
9 London stock (second)
10 Wire cut blue
11 Red common
12 Coarse fletton
13 Molded fletton
14 Drag wire multired

Pattern formed by projecting headers

Decorative combination of colored bricks

Second-hand molded bricks

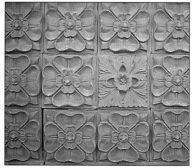

Sometimes whole panels are available

Weathered antique bricks are popular

Buying concrete blocks

When the blocks are delivered, have them unloaded as near as possible to the construction site to save time and reduce the possibility of damage in transit—they are quite brittle and chip easily. Stack them on a flat, dry base and protect them from rain and frost with a tarpaulin or a polyethelene sheet.

Sizes of structural blocks
The nominal size of a block refers to the length and height only, including the mortar joints. But block thicknesses are always specified as the actual size.

Available sizes

Standard blocks are nominally 16 inches long by 8 inches high by 8 inches thick. Many other sizes are available as well, including half and three-quarter units. Available shapes vary widely: Units with keyed ends are used in ordinary wall construction and square-end blocks are used for corners. Single and double bullnose units can be used for decorative designs, and other blocks are made for doorjambs and lintels.

Estimating quantities

To calculate the number required, you must divide a given area of wall by the dimensions of a specific type of block. Blocks are sometimes specified with the mortar joints on the ends, and on the top and bottom. This generally adds ⅜ inch to both dimensions. Because concrete blocks are almost always laid in single courses, the thickness of the block is always specified as the actual dimension.

Screen block

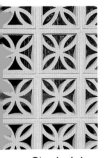

Pilaster block

Standard sizes
Decorative screen blocks are usually 1 foot square and 3½ inches thick.

Screen blocks

Pierced concrete blocks are used for building decorative screens. The blocks are not bonded like brickwork or structural blocks and therefore require supporting piers made from matching pilaster blocks. These are made with channels that hold the sides of the pierced blocks. Solid blocks finish the tops of the screen blocks and piers.

Screen blocks should not be used to build loadbearing walls. However, they can support lightweight structures, like garden arbors.

Choosing concrete blocks

Cast concrete blocks were introduced as a cheap substitute for bricks that were to be covered with plaster or stucco, but they have long since overtaken brick for any number of applications—especially for foundation work. They come in a wide variety of sizes, shapes, colors, and textures and can be used just about anywhere.

Types of block

Lightweight concrete blocks

Made from aerated concrete, these blocks can be carried easily in one hand, which enables masons to build walls quickly and safely. Aerated blocks can be drilled and cut to shape easily, using common hand and power tools. They are used extensively for the construction of both internal and external walls.

Standard concrete blocks

Made from relatively heavy concrete, these are also known as dense concrete blocks. Most of these blocks are nearly hollow on the inside; they just have supporting ribs between the two outer faces. This makes the blocks lighter and provides a hollow space in which to install reinforcing bars (rebars) and concrete.

Varieties of block

Structural blocks

Simple rectangular blocks, cement gray or white in color, are most often used for foundation work. They cost less than bricks and are much faster to install. Another common use of these simple blocks is in the structural core of a wall that will be covered with stucco or plaster later. These blocks are often made with a zigzag keyed surface that allows the finish material to grip the surface better.

Facing blocks

These are blocks with one decorative face for walls that will be entirely exposed. They are often made to resemble natural stone by including some crushed stone aggregate in the mix or by creating a rough, textured surface.

These blocks are used for covering the surface of a structural block wall or for freestanding landscape walls. A wide variety of shapes, sizes, colors, and surface textures is available.

Qualities of block

Loadbearing blocks

Structural blocks are used to construct the loadbearing walls of a building, typically the perimeter foundation walls and occasionally an interior loadbearing wall that supports a central beam. In some situations, lightweight aerated concrete blocks can be used. Generally, though, foundation work calls for standard dense concrete blocks.

Nonloadbearing blocks

These blocks are used to build internal dividing partitions. They are either lightweight aerated blocks or low-density foam concrete blocks. They are easy to handle and install but are rarely used in loadbearing applications.

Insulating blocks

Foamed concrete blocks are often used in commercial applications for the interior side of a standard concrete or concrete-block wall. They have good insulating properties and frequently meet the minimum building code requirements for wall R-values without the need to add secondary insulation.

Newer ultralight foam blocks offer even higher R-values, and some residential foundation systems use these blocks exclusively. They are laid up dry, their cores are filled with concrete, and the outside is parged.

Stone: natural and artificial   ## Choosing stone

Natural stone
Whether it's roughly hewn or finely dressed, natural stone is durable and weathers beautifully.

Artificial-stone wall
(below)
Cast concrete blocks that simulate real stonework are used to construct attractive walls and planters.

Slate-effect wall
(below right)
Good-quality concrete blockwork is difficult to distinguish from real stone once it has weathered. What look like thin pieces of slate are actually cast as large interlocking blocks that can be laid quickly.

Artificial stone blocks, made from poured concrete, can look very convincing, especially after they've weathered. Depending on where you live, these blocks may be easier to obtain than natural building stone and are usually cheaper. But, from the standpoint of pure appearance, nothing can surpass a quarried stone such as granite or sandstone.

Natural stone

Limestone, sandstone, and granite are all suitable materials for building walls. Slate and other flat stones are commonly used for walkways and garden paths but can also be used for walls.

Stone bought in its natural state (undressed) is classified as random rubble. It is perfect for building dry-stone walls in both formal and informal settings. For more regular appearance, ask for semidressed stone, which is cut into reasonably uniform blocks but still has uneven surfaces. Fully dressed stone has flat surfaces cut by a machine. The cost of stone increases in proportion to the degree of preparation it has undergone.

In practical terms, the type of stone you can use for walls depends almost entirely on where you happen to live. The cost of shipping for large quantities of stone from far away is prohibitively high for most people. Besides, a structure built from indigenous stone is more likely to fit in well with the prevailing architecture in your area.

Where to obtain stone

If you live in or very near a city, obtaining natural stone can be a problem. You may be able to easily buy a few small boulders for a rock garden from a local garden center, but the cost of buying enough natural stone for even a short wall can be prohibitive. If you don't want to use artificial stone made from cast concrete, you can rent a truck, drive to the nearest quarry, and transport the stone yourself.

Another source of material is a demolition site. This is usually the cheapest approach, though prices for this material can vary greatly. And you not only have to rent a truck but must also be prepared for a lot of hard work loading and unloading the stone.

Estimating quantities

Most quarries sell stone by the ton. When you have worked out the dimensions of the wall, visit the nearest quarry and look at the different stone they have available. Get their advice on the quantity of stone you'll need for your job and quotes for the cost of the stone if they deliver it, or if you pick it up.

Semidressed, natural stone blocks

Dry-stone retaining wall

Flat stone wall

Undressed stone boundary wall

Artificial-stone blocks

The outside faces of concrete blocks made specifically for garden use are textured to resemble natural stone. These blocks can be laid dry on top of a simple mortar base or bonded together with mortar like conventional stonework. Artificial stone is available in undressed, semidressed, and fully dressed units.

When you are building a wall, mortar is used to bind together the bricks, concrete blocks, or stones. The durability of the wall depends to a large extent upon the quality of the mortar used in its construction. If it's mixed correctly, mortar is strong yet flexible. But if the ingredients are in the wrong proportions, the mortar is likely to be weak or so hard that it is prone to cracking. If too much water is added to the mix, the mortar will be squeezed out of the joints by the weight of the masonry. If the mortar is too dry, then adhesion will be poor.

Bricklayers use a number of specialized words and phrases to describe their craft and materials. Terms used frequently are listed below; others are described as they occur.

BRICK FACES The surfaces of a brick
Stretcher faces—the long sides of a brick
Header faces—the short ends of a brick
Bedding faces—the top and bottom surfaces
Frog—the depression in one bedding face

COURSE A horizontal row of bricks
Stretcher course—a single course with stretcher faces visible
Header course—a single course with header faces visible
Coping—the top course designed to protect the wall from rainwater
Bond—the pattern produced by staggering alternate courses so that vertical joints are not aligned one above the other
Stretcher—a single brick from a stretcher course
Header—a single brick from a header course
Closure brick—the last brick laid in a course

CUT BRICKS Bricks cut to even up the bond
Bat—a brick cut across its width (e.g., half-bat, three-quarter bat)
Queen closer—a brick cut along its length

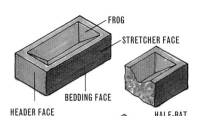

FROG
STRETCHER FACE
BEDDING FACE
HEADER FACE
HALF-BAT

The ingredients of mortar

General-purpose mortar is usually mixed on site from bulk materials. It's made from portland cement, hydrated lime, and sand mixed together with enough water to make a workable paste.

Cement is the hardening agent that binds the other ingredients together. The lime slows down the drying process and prevents the mortar from setting too quickly. It also makes the mix flow well so that it fills gaps in the masonry and adheres to the texture of blocks or bricks. Sand acts as an aggregate, adding body to the mortar and reducing the possibility of shrinkage. For general-purpose mortar, fine builder's sand is ideal.

Plasticizers If you're laying masonry in a period of cold weather, substitute a plasticizer for the lime. Plasticizer produces an aerated mortar in which the tiny air bubbles allow water to expand in freezing conditions, thus reducing the risk of cracking. Premixed masonry cement, which has an aerating agent, is ready for mixing with sand.

Ready-mixed mortar This type of mortar contains all the essential ingredients mixed to the correct proportions—you simply add water. It is a more expensive way of buying mortar, but it's convenient to use and available in small quantities.

Mixing mortar

Mortar should be discarded if it isn't used within two hours of being mixed, so make only as much as you can use within that time. An average of about two minutes for laying each brick is a reasonable estimate.

Choose a flat site to mix the materials—a sheet of plywood will do—and dampen it slightly to prevent it from absorbing water from the mortar. Make a pile of half the amount of sand to be used, then add the other ingredients. Put the rest of the sand on top and mix the dry materials thoroughly.

Scoop a depression in the pile and add clean tap water. Never use contaminated or salty water. Push the dry mix from around the edge of the pile into the water until it has absorbed enough for you to blend the mix with a shovel, using a chopping action. Add more water, little by little, until the mortar has a butterlike consistency, slipping easily from the shovel but firm enough to hold its shape if you make a hollow in the mix. If the sides of the hollow collapse, add more dry ingredients until the mortar firms up. Make sure the mortar is sufficiently moist; dry mortar won't form a strong bond with the masonry.

If the mortar stiffens up while you are working, add just enough water to restore the consistency.

Proportions for masonry mixes

Mix the ingredients according to the prevailing conditions at the building site. Use a general-purpose mortar for moderate conditions where the wall is reasonably sheltered. A stronger mix is required for severe conditions where the wall will be exposed to wind and driving rain, or if the site is elevated or near the coast. If you are using plasticizer rather than lime, follow the manufacturer's instructions regarding the quantity you should add to the sand.

● **Estimating quantity**
As a rough guide to estimating how much mortar you will need when building a wall, allow approximately 1 cubic yard of sand (other ingredients in proportion) to lay about 1600 bricks.

● **Masonry cement**
A ready-mixed cement that is used without adding lime or plasticizer.

MORTAR MIXING PROPORTIONS	Cement/lime mortar	Plasticized mortar	Masonry-cement/mortar
General-purpose mortar (Moderate conditions)	1 part cement 1 part lime 6 parts sand	1 part cement 6 parts sand/ plasticizer	1 part masonry cement 5 parts sand
Strong mortar (Severe conditions)	1 part cement ½ part lime 4 parts sand	1 part cement 4 parts sand/ plasticizer	1 part masonry cement 3 parts sand

Bonding brickwork

Stretcher bond

Flemish bond

Honeycomb bond

Although mortar is extremely strong under compression, its tensile strength is relatively weak. If bricks were stacked one upon the other, so that the vertical joints were continuous, any movement within the wall would pull the joints apart and the structure would be seriously weakened. Bonding the brickwork staggers the vertical joints, transmitting the load along the entire length of the wall. Try out the bond of your choice by dry-laying a few bricks before you embark upon building the wall.

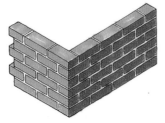

Stretcher bond The stretcher bond is the simplest form of bonding. It is used for single-thickness walls in many different applications from facing walls on wood-framed houses to retaining walls and boundary walls in the yard. Half-bats are used to complete the bond at the end of a straight wall, while a corner is formed by alternating headers and stretchers.

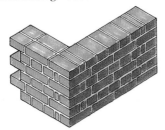

English bond If you were to build a wall 8½ inches thick by laying courses in a stretcher bond side by side, there would be a weak vertical joint running centrally down the wall. An English bond strengthens the wall by using alternate courses of headers. Staggered joints are maintained at the end of the wall and at right-angle corners by

inserting a queen closer before the last header.

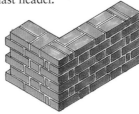

Flemish bond The Flemish bond is another method used for building a solid wall 8½ inches thick. Every course is laid with alternate headers and stretchers. Stagger the joint at the end of a course and at corners by laying a queen closer before the header.

Decorative bonds
Stretcher, English, and Flemish bonds are designed to construct strong walls; decorative qualities are incidental. Other bonds, used primarily for their visual effect, are suitable for low, nonloadbearing walls only. They need to be supported by a conventionally bonded base and by piers.

Stack bonding Laying bricks in groups of three creates a basket-weave effect. Strengthen the continuous vertical joints with wall ties.
Honeycomb bond Build an open decorative screen by using a stretcher-like bond with a quarter-bat-size space between each brick. This type of screen has to be built with care in order to keep the bond regular. Cut quarter-bats to fill the gaps in the top course.

It is easy enough to appreciate the loads and stresses imposed upon the walls of a house or outbuilding, and hence the need for solid foundations with adequate methods of reinforcement and protection to prevent them from collapsing. But it is not so obvious that even a simple garden wall requires similar measures to ensure its stability. It's merely irritating if a low dividing wall or planter falls apart, but a serious injury could result from the collapse of a heavy boundary wall.

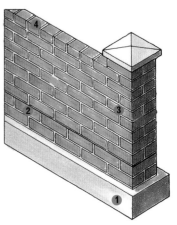

The basic structure of a wall
Unless you design and build a wall in the correct manner, it will not be strong and stable.

Footings
A wall must be built upon a solid concrete platform known as a footing. The dimensions of the footing vary according to the height and weight of the wall.

Bonding
The staggered pattern of the bricks is not merely decorative. It's designed primarily to spread the static load along the wall and to tie the individual bricks together.

Piers
Straight walls that exceed a certain height and length must be buttressed at regular intervals with thick columns of brickwork, known as piers. These resist the sideways pressure caused by high winds.

Coping
The coping prevents frost damage by shedding rainwater from the top of the wall, where it could seep into the upper brick joints.

Sloping sites

Footings for garden walls

If the ground slopes gently, simply ignore the gradient and make footings perfectly level. If the site slopes noticeably, make a stepped footing by placing plywood form stops across the trench at regular intervals. Calculate the height and length of the steps, using multiples of normal brick size.

Support plywood form stops with stakes

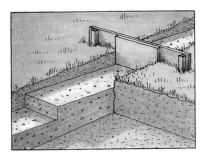

Section through a stepped footing
A typical stepped concrete footing, with one of the plywood form stops in place.

Your local building department establishes the size and reinforcement of the footings required to support masonry walls, especially loadbearing walls. Usually garden walls can be built on concrete footings laid in a simple trench with straight sides.

Size of footings

A footing needs to be substantial enough to support the weight of the wall. The surrounding soil must be firm and well drained to avoid possible subsidence. It's not a good idea to set footings in ground that has been backfilled recently, such as a new building site. Take care to avoid tree roots and drainpipes.

Dig the trench deeper than the footing itself so that the first one or two courses of brick are below ground level. This will allow for an adequate depth of soil for planting right up to the wall.

If the soil is not firmly packed when you reach the required depth, dig deeper until you reach a firm level. Then fill the bottom of the trench with compacted gravel up to the lowest level of the proposed footing.

RECOMMENDED DIMENSIONS FOR FOOTINGS			
Type of wall	Height of wall	Depth of footing	Width of footing
One brick thick	Up to 3 feet	4 to 6 inches	12 inches
Two bricks thick	Up to 3 feet	9 to 12 inches	18 inches
Two bricks thick	Between 3 and 6 feet	16 to 18 inches	18 to 24 inches
Retaining wall	Up to 3 feet	6 to 12 inches	16 to 18 inches

Setting out the footings

For a straight footing, set up two form boards (see below right), made from ¾-inch-thick lumber nailed to stakes that are driven into the ground at each end of the proposed trench. Position outside the work area.

Drive nails into the top edge of each board and stretch lines between them to mark the front and back edges of the wall. Then drive nails into the boards on each side of the wall lines to indicate the width of the footing and stretch other lines between these nails (1).

When you're satisfied that the layout is accurate, remove the lines marking the wall. But leave their nails in place so that you can replace the lines when you come to lay the bricks.

Place a level against the remaining lines to mark the edge of the footing on the ground (2). Mark the ends of the footing, which should extend beyond the end of the wall by half the wall's thickness. Before you remove the lines, mark out each edge of the trench on the ground, using a spade. Leave the form boards in place.

Turning corners If your wall is going to have a right-angled corner, set up two sets of profile boards. Check carefully that the lines form a true right angle, using the 3-4-5 right-triangle method (3).
Digging the trench Excavate the trench, keeping the sides vertical, and check that the bottom is level, using a long straight piece of wood and a level.

Drive a stake into the bottom of the trench near one end until the top of the stake represents the depth of the footing. Drive in more stakes at about 3-foot intervals and check that tops are level (4).
Filling the trench Mix up the concrete, then pour it into the trench. Trowel the surface until it is exactly level with the top of the stakes. Leave the stakes in place and allow the footing to harden thoroughly before laying up the wall.

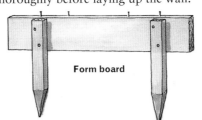

Form board

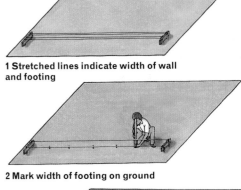

1 Stretched lines indicate width of wall and footing

2 Mark width of footing on ground

3 A triangle measuring 3, 4, and 5 units makes a right angle

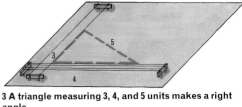

4 Check that tops of stakes are level

Laying bricks

Bricklaying tools

Spreading a bed of mortar requires practice before you can do it at speed – so at first concentrate on laying bricks accurately. Using mortar of exactly the right consistency helps to keep the visible faces of the bricks clean. In hot, dry weather, dampen the footings and bricks before you begin but let any surface water evaporate before you lay the bricks.

Basic bricklaying techniques

Hold the trowel with your thumb in line with the handle and pointing toward the tip of the blade (1).

Scoop some mortar out of the pile and shape it roughly to match the dimensions of the trowel blade. Pick up the mortar by sliding the blade under the pile, settling the mortar onto the trowel with a slight jerk of the wrist (2).

Spread the mortar along the top course by aligning the edge of the trowel with the centerline of the bricks. As you tip the blade to deposit the mortar, draw the trowel back toward you to stretch the bed over at least two to three bricks (3). Furrow the mortar by pressing the point of the trowel along the center of the bed (4).

Pick up a brick with your other hand (5) but don't extend your thumb too far onto the stretcher face or it will disturb the mason's line (see opposite) as you place the brick in position. Press the brick into the bed, picking up excess mortar squeezed from the joint by sliding the edge of the trowel along the face of the wall (6).

Spread mortar onto the header of the next brick, making a neat ⅜-inch bed for the header joint (7). Press the brick against its neighbor, scooping off excess mortar with the trowel.

Having laid three bricks, use a level to check that they are flat and level. Make any adjustments by tapping them down with the trowel handle (8).

Hold the level along the outer edge of the bricks to check that they are in line. To move a brick sideways without knocking it off its mortar bed, tap the upper edge with the trowel at about 45 degrees (9).

Tools for basic bricklaying
While you can improvise some of the tools you need, you should buy the specialized mason's tools shown here to get the best results.

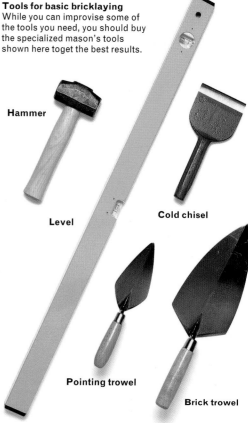

Hammer

Cold chisel

Level

Pointing trowel

Brick trowel

1 The correct way to hold a brick trowel

4 Furrow mortar with point of trowel

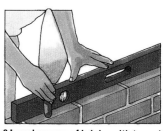

7 Spread mortar onto head of next brick

Cutting bricks
To cut brick, use a cold chisel to mark the line on all faces by tapping gently with a hammer. Realign the blade on the visible stretcher face and strike the chisel firmly.

● **Brick cleaner**
Wash mortar off your tools as soon as the job is finished.

2 Scoop some mortar onto trowel

5 Pick up brick with your thumb on edge

8 Level course of bricks with trowel handle

3 Spread bed of mortar along course

6 Push brick down and remove excess mortar

9 Tap bricks sideways to align them

Building a stretcher-bond wall

Over a certain height, a single-width brick wall is structurally weak unless it either is supported with piers or changes direction by forming right-angle corners. The ability to construct accurate right-angle corners is a requirement for building most structures, even simple garden planters.

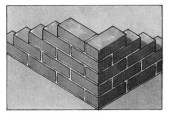

A stepped lead for a corner

Setting out the corners

Mark out the footings and the face of the wall by stretching string lines between form boards. When the footings have been filled and the concrete has set, either use a plumb line or hold a level lightly against the lines to mark the corners and the face of the wall on the footing **(1)**. Join up the marks on the concrete, using a pencil and a straight board, then check the accuracy of the corners with a builder's square. Finally, check that the alignment is straight by stretching a string line between the corner marks.

Building corners

Construct the corners first, as a series of steps. Spread a bed of mortar on the footing and then lay three bricks in both directions against the marked line. Using a level, make sure the bricks are level in all directions, including across the diagonal **(2)**.

Build the corners to a height of five stepped courses, using a marked gauge stick to measure the height of each course as you proceed **(3)**. Use alternate headers and stretchers to form the actual point of the corner.

Plumb the corner and check the alignment of the stepped bricks by holding a level against the sides of the wall **(4)**.

Building the straight sections

Stretch a mason's line between the corners so that it aligns perfectly with the top of the first course **(5)**.

Lay the first straight course of bricks from both ends toward the middle. As you near the middle point, lay the last few bricks dry to make certain they will fit. If necessary, cut the central or closure brick to fit. Mortar the bricks in place and finish by spreading mortar onto both ends of the closure brick and onto the header faces of the bricks on each side **(6)**. Scoop off excess mortar with the trowel. Lay subsequent courses between the leads in the same way, raising the mason's line each time.

To build the wall higher, raise the corners first to the required height and then fill in between with bricks.

Mason's line
Bricklayers use a nylon line as a guide for keeping bricks level. The line is stretched between two flat nails that are driven into vertical joints at each end of the wall.

Coping the wall
You could finish the wall by laying the last course frog side down. Or use a series of half-bats laid on end to get a more professional look.

● **Protecting a wall**
To protect the brickwork from rain or frost, cover newly built walls overnight with a tarp or sheets of polyethylene. Weight down the edges of the covers with bricks.

4 Check that steps are in line

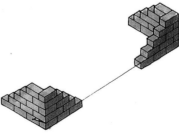

5 Stretch a mason's line along first course

2 Level first course of bricks

1 Mark face of wall on footing

3 Check height with gauge stick

6 Lay the last, or closure, brick carefully

Pointing brickwork

Flush joint

Rubbed joint

V-joint

Raked joint

Weatherstruck joint

● **Colored mortar**
You can change the appearance of mortar by adding colored powder to the mix. Make a trial batch to see how it looks when the mortar is dry.

When you are ready to point the brickwork, rake out the joints and refill them with the colored mortar. Work carefully to avoid staining the bricks.

Pointing the mortar between the bricks makes for packed, watertight joints and also enhances the appearance of the wall. Well-struck joints and clean bricks are essential for the wall to look professionally built. For best results, the mortar must be shaped when it has just the right consistency.

Consistency of the mortar

If the mortar is still too wet, the joint will not be crisp and you may drag mortar out from between the bricks. On the other hand, if it's left to harden too long, pointing will be difficult and you may leave dark marks on the joint.

Test the consistency of the mortar by pressing your thumb into a joint. If it holds a clear impression without sticking to your thumb, the mortar is just right for pointing. Because it's important to start shaping the joints at exactly the right moment, you may have to point the work in stages before you can complete the wall. Shape the joints to match existing brickwork or choose a profile that is suitable for the prevailing weather conditions.

Shaping the mortar joints

Flush joint After using the edge of your trowel to scrape the mortar flush, stipple the joints with a stiff bristle brush to expose the sand aggregate.
Concave (rubbed) joint Buy a shaped jointing tool to make a rubbed joint or improvise with a length of bent tubing. Scrape the mortar flush first, then drag the

tool along the joints. Finish the vertical joints, then shape the horizontal ones. This is a utilitarian joint, ideal for a wall built with secondhand bricks that are not good enough to take a crisp joint.
V-joint Produced in a similar way to the rubbed joint, the V-joint gives a very sharp finish to new brickwork and sheds rainwater well.
Raked joint Use a piece of wood or metal to rake out the joints to a depth of about ¼ inch. Then compress them again by smoothing the mortar lightly with the end of a wood dowel. Raked joints do not shed water, so they are not suitable for an exposed site.
Weatherstruck joint The angled weatherstruck joint will withstand harsh conditions. Use a small pointing trowel to shape the vertical joints **(1)**. They can slope to the left or right, but be consistent.

Shape the horizontal joints, allowing the mortar to spill out slightly at the base of each joint. Finish the joint by cutting off excess mortar with a tool called a Frenchman, which is like a table knife with its tip bent at 90 degrees. You can improvise one by bending a strip of metal. Make a neat, straight edge to the mortar, using a board aligned with the bottom of each joint to guide the tool **(2)**. Nail two scraps of wood to the board to hold it away from the wall.
Cleaning the brickwork Let the shaped joints harden a little before cleaning scraps of mortar from the face of the wall with a medium-soft brush. Sweep the brush lightly across the joints to avoid damaging the mortar.

The coping—which forms the top course of the wall—protects the brickwork from weathering and gives the wall a finished appearance.

Technically, a coping that is flush with both faces of the wall is called a capping. A true coping projects from the face so that water drips clear and doesn't leave a stain on the brickwork.

Finish a wall with a coping of matching bricks or create a pleasing contrast with differently colored or textured bricks. You can also buy special coping bricks that are designed to shed rainwater more efficiently than other bricks.

Stone or cast concrete slabs are popular for coping walls. Both are quick to lay and when installed on low walls can form comfortable bench seating.

On an exposed site, consider installing a tile and brick coping. This design is eye-catching and protects the wall by shedding rainwater away from most of the bricks.

Brick coping
Specially shaped coping bricks are designed to shed rainwater.

Slab coping
Choose a stone or concrete slab that is wider than the wall itself.

Tile and brick coping
Lay flat roof tiles beneath a coping of bricks. The projecting tiles shed water clear of the wall.

1 Shape weatherstruck joint with trowel

2 Remove excess mortar with Frenchman

Shape mortar with jointing tool

Building intersecting walls

When building new walls that intersect at right angles, either join them by bonding the brickwork (see below) or take the easier option and link them with wall ties at every third course. If the intersecting wall is more than 6 feet long, make the junction a control joint by using straight metal strips as wall ties.

Building up to a wall

Some brick house walls have what is called a damp-proof course (DPC). This consists of a layer of impervious material built into the mortar bed about 6 inches above ground level. When you build a new wall that intersects with a house wall that has a DPC, you should include a DPC in the new wall. Use a roll of bituminous roofing felt that matches the thickness of the new wall.

First, locate the house's DPC and build the first few courses of the new wall up to that level. Then spread a thin bed of mortar on the bricks and lay the DPC on it with the end of the roll turned up against the existing wall **(1)**. The next course of bricks will trap the DPC between the end brick and the house wall. Lay more mortar on top of the DPC to produce a standard ⅜-inch-thick joint, ready for laying the next course in the normal way. If you have to join rolls of felt, overlap the ends by at least 6 inches.

Tying in the new wall The traditional method for linking a new wall with an existing structure involves chopping recesses in the brickwork at every fourth course. End bricks of the new wall are set into the recesses, bonding the two structures together **(2)**. However, a simpler method is to bolt to the wall a special stainless-metal connector, which is designed to anchor bricks or concrete blocks, using special wall ties. Standard connectors will accommodate walls from 4 to 10 inches thick.

Bolt a connector to the old wall, just above the DPC, if one exists **(3)**. Use anchor bolts recommended by the connector-plate manufacturer.

Mortar the end of a brick before laying it against the connector **(4)**. At every third course, hook a wall tie into one of the lugs in the connector and bed each tie in the mortar joint **(5)**.

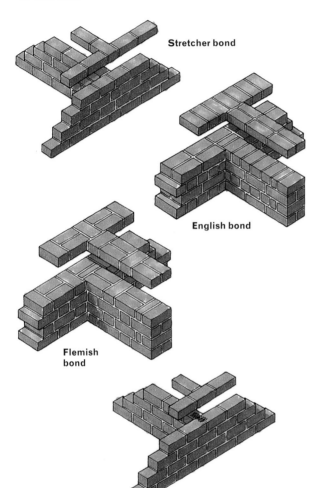

Stretcher bond

English bond

Flemish bond

Using a wall tie

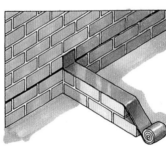

1 Lap existing DPC with new roll

3 But it is easier to use a special connector

2 Interlock new wall with existing wall

4 Lay bricks against connector

5 Bed special wall tie in mortar joint

Wall connector ties

29

Brick piers

Bonding piers

A pier is a freestanding column of masonry that is used for such things as a support for a porch or a pergola or to form an individual gatepost. When a column is built as part of a wall, it is more accurately termed a pilaster. In practice, however, the word column is often used to mean either structure. To avoid confusion, any supporting brick column will be described here as a pier.

Structural considerations

A freestanding wall over a certain length and height must be reinforced at regular intervals by piers. The straight sections of wall have to be tied to the piers, either by a brick bond or by inserting metal wall ties in every third course of bricks.

Whatever its height, any single-width brick wall would benefit from supporting piers at each end and at gateways, where it is most vulnerable. Piers also serve to improve the appearance of this type of wall.

Piers that are more than 3 feet high, especially those supporting gates, should be built around steel reinforcing rods set in the concrete footings. Whether reinforcing is included or not, allow for the size of the piers when planning any footings.

Designing the piers

Piers should be placed no more than 10 feet apart in walls over a certain height (see chart below). The wall itself can be flush with one face of each pier, but the structure is stronger if the wall is centered on the piers.

Piers should be a minimum of twice the thickness of a wall that is 4 inches thick. But build piers 14 inches square to buttress a wall 8 inches thick or when reinforcement is required, such as for gates.

If you prefer the appearance of bonded brick piers, construct them as shown below. It is easier, however, to use wall ties to reinforce continuous vertical joints in the brickwork, especially when building walls centered on piers.

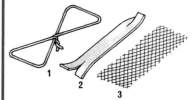

Wall ties
Various types of galvanized-metal wall ties are available: wire bent into a butterfly shape **(1)**, stamped steel strips with forked ends, known as fish tails **(2)**, and expanded-metal mesh strips **(3)**.

Bonding piers
While it's simpler to tie a wall to a pier with wall ties, it's relatively easy to bond a pier into a wall that is a single brick wide.

Color key
You will have to cut certain bricks to bond a pier into a straight wall. Whole bricks are colored with a light tone, three-quarter bats with a medium tone, and half-bats with a dark tone.

INCORPORATING PIERS IN A BRICK WALL		
Thickness of wall	Maximum height without piers	Maximum pier spacing
4 inches	18 inches	10 feet
8 inches	4 feet 6 inches	10 feet

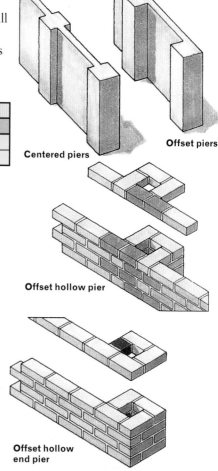

Centered piers

Offset piers

Offset hollow pier

Offset hollow end pier

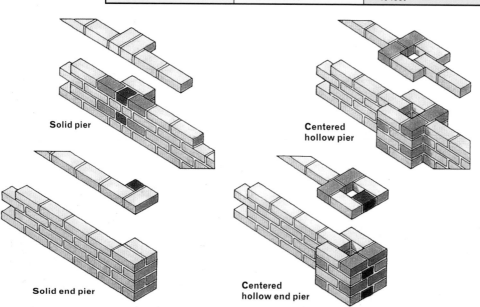

Solid pier

Centered hollow pier

Solid end pier

Centered hollow end pier

Control joints

Although it's not noticeable, a brick wall moves from time to time as a result of ground settlement and expansion and contraction of the materials. Over short distances the movement is so slight that it has hardly any effect on the brickwork, but in a long wall it can crack the structure.

To compensate for this movement, build continuous mortar-free vertical joints into the wall at intervals of about 20 feet. Although these control joints can be placed in a straight section of wall, it is neater and more convenient to place them where the wall meets a pier. In this situation, build the pier and the wall as usual but omit the mortar from the header joints of the wall. Instead of inserting standard wall ties, embed a flat galvanized strip in the mortar bed. Lightly grease one half of the strip with automotive grease or petroleum jelly so that it can slide lengthwise to allow for movement and yet still key the wall and the pier together. When the wall is complete, fill the joint from both sides with caulk.

Adding reinforcement

Use ⅝-inch steel reinforcing bars to strengthen brick piers. If the pier is less than 3 feet high, use a single continuous length of bar **(1)**. For taller piers, embed a bent starter bar in the footing, projecting a minimum of 20 inches above the level of the concrete. As the work proceeds, use galvanized wire to bind extension bars to the starter bars **(2)**, up to 2 inches below the top of the pier. Fill in around the rebar with concrete as you build the pier. Pack the concrete very carefully so that you don't disturb the brickwork.

Control joint

Making a control joint
When making a control joint, tie the pier to the wall with galvanized-metal strips, shown here before the bed of mortar is laid. Caulk is squeezed into the vertical joint between the wall and the pier.

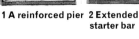

BRICK PIER
REBAR

CONCRETE FILL

FOOTING

1 A reinforced pier 2 Extended starter bar

On the concrete footing, accurately mark out the positions of the piers and the face of the wall. Lay the first course of bricks for the piers, using a mason's line stretched between two stakes to align them **(1)**. Adjust the position of the line if necessary, and fill in between with the first straight course, working from both ends toward the middle **(2)**. Build alternate pier and wall courses, checking that the bricks are laid level and the faces and corners of the piers are vertical. At every third course, push metal wall ties into the mortar bed to span the joints between the wall and the piers **(3)**. Continue in the same way to the required height of the wall, then raise the piers by at least one extra course **(4)**. Lay a coping along the wall and cap the piers with concrete or stone slabs **(5)**.

1 Lay pier bases
Stretch a mason's line to position the bases of the piers.

2 Lay first wall course
Use the line to keep the first course of bricks straight.

3 Install pier ties
Join the piers to the wall by inserting wall ties into every third course. Put a tie into every second course for a gate pier.

4 Raise the piers
Build the piers higher than the wall to allow for a decorative coping along the top course.

5 Lay the coping
Lay coping on wall bricks and cap the piers.

Positioning piers
This brick pier has been strategically placed to support the wall and disguise the point where the ground level changes.

Building with concrete blocks   Control joints

Don't dampen concrete blocks before you lay them because wet blocks may shrink and crack the mortar joints as the wall dries out. Block walls need the same type of concrete footings and mortar mixes as brick walls.

Because concrete blocks are made in a greater variety of sizes, you can build a wall of many different thicknesses, using a simple stretcher bond.

Make the mortar joints flush with the surface of a wall that is going to be covered with stucco or plaster. For painted or exposed blocks, point the joints using a style that will enhance the appearance or performance of the wall.

Colorful block walls
High-quality blocks decorated with smooth masonry paint make a welcome change from the usual monotonous gray concrete.

Block types (from top)
Solid top block
Corner block
Basic block
Solid block

Building a partition wall
It is usual to divide up large interior spaces with nonloadbearing stud partitions. But if your house is built on a concrete slab, an alternative is to use concrete blocks.

If you're going to install a doorway in the partition, plan its position to avoid cutting too many blocks. You will need to allow for the wood doorframe, as well as a precast lintel to support the masonry above the opening. Fill the space above the lintel with concrete bricks.

Bolt metal connectors to the existing structure in order to support each end of the new partition wall. Plumb the connectors accurately to make sure the new wall is built perfectly plumb.

Lay the first course of blocks without mortar, across the room, to check their spacing and to determine the position of any doorways. Mark the positions of the blocks before building steps at each end, as explained earlier for brick walls. Check for accuracy with a level, and then fill in between the ends with blocks.

Lay another three courses, anchoring the end blocks to the connectors with wall ties in every joint. Leave the mortar to harden overnight before you continue with the wall.

Building intersecting walls
Butt intersecting walls together with a continuous vertical joint between them, but anchor the structure with wire-mesh wall ties **(1)**. If you build a wall with heavyweight hollow blocks, use heavy metal tie bars with a bend at each end. Fill the block voids with mortar to embed the ends of the bars **(2)**. Install a tie in every course.

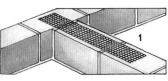
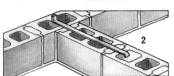

1 Wire-mesh wall ties for solid blocks
2 Metal tie bar for hollow blocks

Cutting blocks
If you don't have a masonry-saw blade, cut a concrete block by scoring a line around it using a cold chisel. Deepen the line into a groove by striking the chisel sharply with hammer, working your way around the block until it eventually fractures along the chiseled groove.

Walls over 20 feet long should be built with a continuous vertical control joint to allow for expansion. Place an unmortared joint in a straight section of wall or against a pier and bridge the gap with galvanized-metal strips, as for brick walls. Fill the vertical joint with flexible caulk.

If you need to insert a control joint in a partition wall, it's convenient to form the joint at a door opening. Install it around one end of the lintel and then vertically to the ceiling. Having filled the joint with mortar in the normal way, rake it out to a depth of ¾ inch on both sides of the wall, then fill the joint flush with caulk.

Forming a control joint next to a door opening
Install the joint around the lintel and up to the ceiling on both sides of the wall.

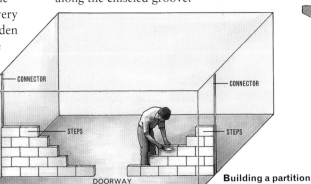

Building a partition

Cutting a block
Use a cold chisel and hammer to cut block.

Cavity walls are used in the construction of buildings to prevent moisture from seeping to the interior. This is achieved by building two independent masonry walls with a gap between them. The gap provides a degree of thermal insulation, but the insulation value increases significantly if you install insulation in the cavity.

The exterior wall of most cavity walls is constructed with bricks. The inner wall is sometimes built with bricks, too, but more often with concrete blocks. Whatever type of masonry is used, both walls must be tied together with wall ties spanning the gap. Cavity walls are likely to be loadbearing, so they have to be built accurately. Hire a professional for this job and make sure he or she avoids dropping mortar into the gap. If mortar collects at the base of the cavity, or even on one of the wall ties, moisture can bridge the gap and enter the interior of the room.

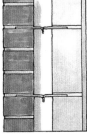

Cavity wall construction
A section through a typical cavity wall built with an exterior wall of bricks tied to an inner wall of plastered concrete blocks.

Reinforcing a high wall
Any screen built higher than 2 feet should be reinforced vertically with ⅝-inch steel rebars. Galvanized mesh strips should be embedded in the horizontal mortar joints.

Basic bricklaying techniques and tools are used to build a pierced concrete screen, but the blocks are stack-bonded with continuous vertical joints.

If a screen wall is to be built higher than 2 feet, it must be reinforced vertically with ⅝-inch steel rebars and horizontally with galvanized mesh strips. Build a screen with supporting piers no more than 10 feet apart, using matching pilaster blocks. If you prefer the appearance of contrasting masonry, construct a base and piers from bricks (see below right).

Constructing a screen

Install concrete footings, making them twice the width of the pilaster blocks. Embed rebars in the concrete and support them with ropes until the concrete sets.

Lower a pilaster block over the first bar, setting it onto a bed of mortar laid around the base of the bar. Check that the block is perfectly plumb and level and that its side channel faces the next pier. Pack mortar or concrete into its core, then proceed with two more blocks so that the pier corresponds to the height of two mortared screen blocks **(1)**. Construct each pier in the same way. Intermediate piers will have a channel on both sides.

Allow the mortar to harden overnight, then lay a mortar bed for two screen blocks next to the first pier. Cover the vertical edge of a screen block with mortar and press it into the pier channel **(2)**. Tap the block into the mortar bed and check that it's level. Mortar the next block and place it alongside the first. When covering screen blocks with mortar, take care to keep the faces clean by making a neat chamfered bed of mortar **(3)**.

Lay two more blocks against the next pier. Stretch a mason's line to gauge the top edge of the first course, then lay the rest of the blocks toward the center, making sure that the vertical joints are aligned perfectly. Before building any higher, embed a wire reinforcing strip running from pier to pier in the next mortar bed **(4)**. Continue to build the piers and screen up to a maximum height of 6 feet 6 inches, inserting a wire strip into alternate courses. Finally, lay coping units on top of each pier and along the top of the screen **(5)**.

If you don't like the appearance of ordinary mortar joints, rake out some of the mortar and repoint with mortar made with silver sand. A concave rubbed joint suits decorative screening.

1 Build piers

2 Fit block to pier

3 Mortar edge of block

4 Lay wire reinforcing strip into mortar

5 Lay coping units along wall

Building with stone

Designing the wall

C onstructing walls with natural stone requires a different approach than building with bricks or concrete blocks. A stone wall has to be as stable as one built with any other masonry product, but its visual appeal relies on the courses being less regular. In fact, it's impossible to have regular courses when a wall is built with undressed stone.

Structural considerations

Not all stone walls are built with mortar, although it is often used with dressed or semidressed stone in order to provide additional stability.

Usually walls are tapered, with heavy, flat stones laid at the base of the wall, followed by proportionally smaller stones as the height increases. This traditional form of construction was developed to prevent walls made with unmortared stones from toppling sideways when subjected to high winds or the weight of farm animals.

Far from detracting from its appearance, this informal construction suits a country style perfectly.

Building a dry-stone wall

As described above, a true dry-stone wall relies on the careful selection and placement of stones to provide stability. However, there's no reason why you can't introduce mortar, particularly within the core of the wall, and still maintain the appearance of dry-stone structure. Another way to help stabilize a wall is to bed the stones in soil, packing it firmly into the crevices as you lay each course. This enables you to add suitable plants to the wall, even during its construction.

When you are selecting the stone, watch for flat stones in a variety of sizes and make sure you have some that are large enough to run the full width of the wall, especially at the

base of the structure. Placed at regular intervals, these bonding stones are important components because they tie the loose stones into a cohesive structure.

Even a low wall will inevitably include some heavy stones. When you lift them, keep your back straight and your feet together, using the muscles of your legs to take the strain.

Constructing the wall

Assuming you're using soil as your joint material, spread a 1-inch layer over the footing and then place a substantial bonding stone across the width to form the bed of the first course (1). Lay other stones, about the same height as the bonding stone, along each side of the wall, pressing them down into the soil to make a firm base. It's worth stretching a mason's line along each side of the wall to help you make a reasonably straight base.

Lay smaller stones between to fill out the base of the wall (2), then pack more soil into all the crevices.

Spread another layer of soil on top of the base and lay a second course of stones, bridging the joints between the stones below (3). Press the stones down firmly, so they lean in toward the center of the wall. As you proceed, check by eye that the course is about level and remember to include bonding stones at regular intervals.

You can introduce plants into

A dry-stone wall must be tapered, beginning with a wide base, followed by stones that slope in toward the middle of the wall.

For a wall about 3½ feet high—it's risky to build a dry-stone wall any higher—the base should be no less than 18 inches wide. And you need to provide a minimum slope of 1 inch for every 2 feet of height.

Traditionally, the base of this type of wall rests on a bed of sand about 4 inches deep. This sand should lay on compacted soil at the bottom of a shallow trench.

For a more reliable foundation, lay a 4-inch concrete footing, making it about 4 inches wider than the wall on each side.

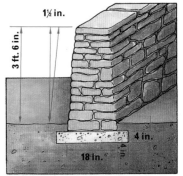

Proportions of stone wall

the larger crevices or hammer smaller stones into the cracks to lock large stones in place (4).

At the top of the wall, either fill the core with soil for plants or lay large, flat coping stones in place. Finally, brush any loose soil from the faces of the stones.

Dry-stone wall
Traditional dry-stone wall is stable without having to fill the joints with mortar.

Pointed stonework
Mortar is required for buildings and substantial freestanding walls constructed from dressed or semidressed stone.

1 Lay wide bonding stone across end of wall

2 Fill out base with small stones

3 Lay second course of stones

4 Fill cracks

Finishing stone walls

When the wall is complete, rake out the joints so that it looks like a traditional dry-stone wall.

An old paintbrush is a useful tool for smoothing the mortar in deep crevices to create firm, watertight joints. It is best to finish regular stone walls with concave rubbed joints.

Allow the mortar to set for a day or two before filling behind the wall. Lay gravel at the base to cover the drainage pipes and firmly pack soil against the rest of the wall. Provide a generous layer of topsoil to finish the backfilling.

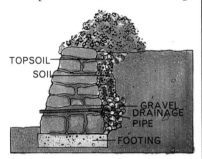

TOPSOIL
SOIL
GRAVEL
DRAINAGE
PIPE
FOOTING

Filling behind a stone wall

Building low retaining walls

Retaining walls are designed to hold back a bank of soil. But don't try to cut into a steep bank and restrain it with a single high wall. Apart from the obvious dangers of the wall collapsing, terracing the slope with a series of low walls is a more sensible solution, which offers opportunities for creative landscaping.

Choosing your materials

Both bricks and concrete blocks make sturdy retaining walls, provided they are reinforced with metal bars buried in a sound concrete footing. Either run the bars through hollow concrete blocks **(1)** or build a double brick wall, like a miniature cavity wall, using wall ties to bind bothh sides together **(2)**.

The mass and weight of natural stone make it ideal for retaining walls. A stone wall should be tapered to an angle of 2 inches for every 1 foot of height, so that the wall actually leans into the bank **(3)**. For safety, don't build higher than 3½ feet.

A skillful builder could construct a perfectly safe dry-stone retaining wall, but unless you have had some experience with this work, it's a better idea to use mortar for more rigidity.

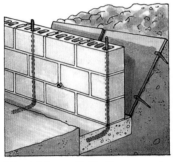

1 A retaining wall of hollow concrete blocks

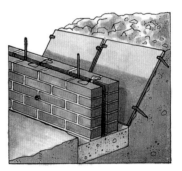

2 Use two walls of brick tied together

3 Lean stone wall against bank of soil

Constructing the wall

Excavate the soil to provide enough room to dig the footing and construct the wall. If the bank is loosely packed, restrain it temporarily with sheets of scrap plywood or similar sheeting. Drive long steel pegs into the bank to hold the sheets in place **(1)**. Install the footing at the base of the bank, and allow it to set before you begin building the wall.

Use conventional techniques to build a block or brick wall. Lay uncut stones as if you were building a dry-stone wall, but set each course on mortar. If you use regular stone blocks, stagger the joints and select stones of different proportions to add variety to the wall. Set the stones in mortar.

You must allow for drainage behind the wall, or else the soil will become water-saturated. So when you lay the second course of stones, embed ¾-inch plastic pipes in the mortar, angling them very slightly toward the base of the wall. Lay the pipes 3 feet apart, making sure that they pass right through the wall and project a little from the face **(2)**.

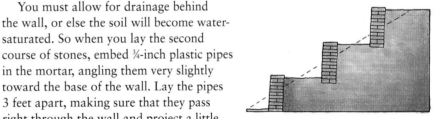

Terracing with retaining walls

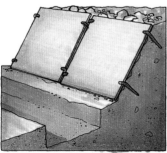

1 Hold back earth with scrap plywood

2 Set plastic pipes in wall for drainage

Masonry maintenance

Before you decorate the outside of your house, check the condition of the brick and stonework and carry out any necessary repairs. There's no reason why you can't paint brick or stonework, but you may want to restore painted masonry to its original condition. Although most paint strippers cannot cope with deeply textured surfaces, there are thick-paste paint removers that will peel away layers of old paint from masonry.

Paint-stained brickwork

Organic growth

Efflorescence

Treating new masonry

New brickwork or stonework should be left for about three months, until it is completely dry, before any further treatment is considered.

White powdery deposits called efflorescence may come to the surface over this period, but you can simply brush them off with a stiff-bristle brush or a piece of rough cloth. New masonry should be weatherproof and should not require further treatment, unless you want to apply paint.

Cleaning off unsightly mold

Colorful lichens growing on garden walls can be very attractive. Indeed, some people actively encourage their growth. However, since the spread of molds and lichens depends on damp conditions, it is not a good sign when they occur naturally on the walls of your house.

Try to identify the source of the problem before treating the growth. For example, if one side of the house never receives any sun, it will have little chance of drying out. Relieve the situation by cutting back overhanging trees or adjacent shrubs to increase ventilation to the wall.

Cracked or corroded gutters and downspouts leaking onto the wall are another common cause of organic growth. Feel behind the pipe with your fingers, or slip a hand mirror behind it to see if there's a leak.

Removing and neutralizing the growth Scrape heavy organic growth from the bricks using a plastic putty knife. Then brush the masonry vigorously with a stiff-bristle brush. This can be an unpleasant, dusty job, so wear a face mask and safety glasses or goggles. Brush away from yourself so that debris doesn't land on your clothes.

Starting at the top of the wall, use a nylon brush to paint on a fungicidal solution, diluted according to the manufacturer's instructions. Apply the fungicide liberally and leave the wall to dry for 24 hours, then rinse the masonry thoroughly with clean water.

In extreme cases, give the wall two washes of fungicide, allowing 24 hours between applications and a further 24 hours before washing it down with clean water.

Removing efflorescence from masonry

Soluble salts within building materials such as cement, brick, and stone gradually migrate to the surface, along with the moisture, as a wall dries out. The result is a white crystalline deposit called efflorescence.

Curing efflorescence
Brush the white deposit from the wall with a stiff-bristle brush or a piece of coarse cloth until the crystals are removed.

The same condition can occur on old masonry if it is subjected to more than average moisture. Efflorescence itself is not harmful, but the source of the damp must be identified and cured.

Brush the deposit from the wall regularly with a dry, stiff-bristle brush or coarse cloth until the crystals cease to form. Don't attempt to wash off the crystals—they will merely dissolve in the water and soak back into the wall. Above all, don't paint a wall that is still efflorescing, as this is a sign that it is still damp.

Masonry paints and clear sealants that let the wall breathe are not affected by the alkali content of the masonry, so they can be used without applying a primer. If you plan to use oil-based paint, coat the wall first with an alkali-resistant primer.

You can often spruce up masonry by washing off surface grime with water. Strong solvents will harm certain types of stone, so consult an experienced mason before applying anything other than water.

Washing the wall
Starting at the top of the wall, use a hose to spray water gently onto the masonry while you scrub it with a stiff-bristle brush **(1)**. Scrub heavy deposits with half a cup of ammonia added to a bucketful of water, then rinse again. Avoid soaking brick or stone when a frost is forecast.

Removing unsightly stains
Soften tar, grease, and oil stains using a household kitchen cleanser. Check package instructions for proper application and rinsing.

Stripping spilled paint
To remove a patch of spilled paint, use paint stripper. Follow the maker's directions and wear old clothes, gloves, and goggles.

Stipple the stripper onto the rough texture **(2)**. Leave it for about 10 minutes, then remove the softened paint with a scraper. Gently scrub the residue out of deeper crevices with a stiff-bristle brush and water. Then rinse the wall with clean water.

If any paint remains in the crevices, dip your brush in stripper and gently scrub it into problem areas. Use small circular strokes. After the stripper has set, wash it off and repeat if necessary.

A combination of frost action and erosion tends to break down the mortar pointing of brickwork and stonework. The mortar eventually falls out, exposing the open joints to wind and rain, which drive dampness through the wall to the inside of the house.

Cracked joints may also be caused by using a hard, inflexible mortar. Replacing defective mortar is a straightforward but time-consuming task. Tackle a small manageable area at a time, using a ready-mixed mortar made for this job.

Applying the mortar
Scrape out the old pointing with a thin wooden stick to a depth of about ½ inch. Use a cold chisel and a hammer to dislodge sections that are firmly embedded; then brush out the joints with a stiff-bristle brush.

Spray the wall with water to make sure the bricks or stones will not absorb too much moisture from the fresh mortar. Mix up some mortar in a bucket and transfer it to a hawk. If you are mixing your own mortar, use these proportions: 1 part cement, 1 part lime, 6 parts builder's sand.

Pick up a small sausage of mortar on the back of a pointing trowel and push it firmly into the upright joints. This can be difficult to do without the mortar dropping off, so hold the hawk under each joint to catch it.

Try not to smear the face of the bricks with mortar, as it will stain. Use the same method for the horizontal joints. The shape of the pointing is not vital at this stage.

Once the mortar is firm enough to retain a thumbprint, it is ready for shaping. Because it is important that you shape the joints at exactly the right moment, you may have to point the work in stages in order to complete the wall. Shape the joints to match existing brickwork, or choose a profile suitable for the prevailing weather conditions in your area.

Once you have shaped the joints, wait until the pointing has almost hardened, then brush the wall to remove traces of surplus mortar from the masonry surface.

Shaping the mortar joints
The joints shown here are commonly used for brickwork. Flush or rubbed joints are best for most stonework, though sometimes raised mortar joints are used with stone. Instructions on producing these profiles are given on page 28.

Colored mortar
Liquid or powder additives are available for changing the color of mortar to match existing pointing. Color matching can be tricky, so make a trial batch to see how it looks when the mortar is dry. Work carefully as smears can stain the bricks permanently.

Mortar dyes
Liquid or powder additives are available for changing the color of mortar to match existing pointing. Color matching can be difficult, and smears can stain the bricks permanently.

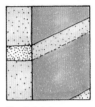
Flush joint

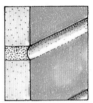
Rubbed joint

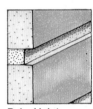
Raked joint

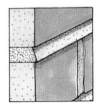
Weatherstruck joint

1 Remove dirt and dust by washing　**2 Stipple paint stripper onto paint**

Repairing masonry

Spalled masonry

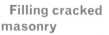

Cracked masonry may simply be the result of cement-rich mortar being unable to absorb slight movements within the building. However, it could also be a sign of a more serious problem—sinking foundations, for example. Don't just ignore the symptoms; investigate immediately and undertake the necessary repairs as soon as possible.

Filling cracked masonry

If a brick or stone wall has substantial cracks, consult a local builder or home inspector to ascertain the cause. If a crack proves to be stable, you can carry out some repairs yourself.

Cracked mortar can be removed and repointed in the normal way, but a crack that splits the bricks cannot be repaired neatly, and the damaged masonry should be replaced by a mason.

Cracks across a painted wall can be filled with mortar that has been mixed with a little bonding agent to help it stick. Before you make the repair, wet the damaged masonry with a hose to encourage the mortar to flow deeply into the crack.

Priming brickwork for painting

Brickwork will need to be primed only if it is showing signs of efflorescence or spalling. An alkali-resistant primer will guard against efflorescence. A stabilizing solution will bind crumbling masonry and also help to seal it.

When you are painting a wall for the first time with masonry paint, you may find that the first coat is difficult to apply due to the suction of the dry, porous brick. Thin the first coat slightly with water or solvent.

Waterproofing masonry

Colorless water-repellent fluids are intended to make masonry impervious to water without coloring it or stopping it from breathing, which is important because it allows moisture within the walls to dry out.

Prepare the surface before applying the fluid: Repair any cracks in bricks or pointing and remove organic growth; then allow the wall to dry out thoroughly. Cover nearby plants.

The fumes from water-repellents can be dangerous if inhaled, so be sure to wear a proper respirator as recommended by the manufacturer. Also, wear eye protection.

Apply the fluid generously with a large paintbrush, from the bottom up, and stipple it into the joints. Apply a second coat as soon as the first has been absorbed to ensure that there are no bare patches where water could seep in. To be sure that you are covering the wall properly, use a sealant containing a fugitive dye, which disappears after a specified period of time.

Carefully paint up to surrounding woodwork. If you accidentally splash sealant onto it, wash it immediately with a cloth dampened with solvent.

If you need to treat a whole house, it may be worth hiring a company that can spray the sealant. Make sure the workers rig up screens to prevent overspray from drifting across to your neighbors' property.

Moisture that has penetrated soft masonry will expand in icy weather, flaking off the outer face of brickwork and stonework. The result, known as spalling, not only looks unattractive but also allows water to seep into the wall.

If spalling is localized, cut out and replace the bricks or stones. The sequence below describes how to repair spalled brickwork, but the process is similar for a stone wall.

Where spalling is extensive, the only practical solution is to accept its less-than-perfect appearance, repoint the masonry, and apply a clear water-repellent that will protect the wall from further damage while allowing it to breathe.

Replacing a spalled brick

Use a cold chisel and hammer to remove the pointing surrounding the brick, then chop out the brick itself. If the brick is difficult to remove, drill numerous holes in it with a large-diameter masonry bit; then chop out the brick with a cold chisel and hammer. It should crumble, enabling you to remove the pieces easily.

To fit the replacement brick, first dampen the opening and spread mortar on the base and one side. Then dampen the replacement brick, cover the top and one end with mortar, and slot the brick into the hole (see far left). Shape the pointing to match the surrounding brickwork.

If you can't find a replacement brick in the right color, remove the spalled brick carefully, turn it around to the undamaged side, and reinsert it.

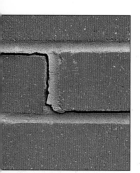
Cracks may follow mortar only

Cracked bricks could signify serious faults

Replacing a spalled brick Having mortared the top and one end, slip the new brick into the hole you have cut.

Spalled bricks caused by frost damage

Exterior masonry paints

Cement paint

Cement paint is supplied as a dry powder to which water is added. It is based on white cement, but pigments are added to produce a range of colors. Cement paint is one of the cheaper paints suitable for exterior use. Spray new or porous surfaces with water, then apply two coats.

Mixing cement paint Shake or roll the container to loosen the powder, then add two parts of powder to one part of water in a clean bucket. Stir it to a smooth paste, then add a little more water until you get a full-bodied, creamy consistency. Don't mix more than you can use in an hour or it will start to dry.

Adding an aggregate When you're painting a wall that has been treated with a stabilizing solution so its porosity is substantially reduced, add clean sand to the mix to give it body. This also provides added protection for an exposed wall and helps to cover dark colors. If the sand changes the color of the paint, add it to the first coat only. Use one part sand to four parts of powder, stirring it in when the paint is still in a pastelike consistency.

Masonry paints

Exterior-masonry paints come in a smooth matte finish or with a fine granular texture.

Water-based masonry paint Most masonry paints are water based, with additives that prevent mold growth. Although they are sold ready for use, on porous walls it pays to thin the first coat with 20 percent water. Follow up with one or two full-strength coats, depending on the color of the paint.

Water-based masonry paints must be applied during fairly good weather. Damp or humid conditions and low temperatures may prevent the paint from drying properly.

Solvent-based masonry paints Some masonry paints are thinned with mineral spirits or with a special solvent. But unlike most oil paints they are moisture-vapor permeable, so that the wall is able to breathe. It is often best to thin the first coat with 15 percent mineral spirits, but check the manufacturer's recommendations. Solvent-based paints can be applied in practically any weather conditions, provided it is not actually raining.

Reinforced masonry paint Masonry paint that has powdered mica or a similar fine aggregate added to it dries with a textured finish that is extremely weatherproof. Although large cracks and holes must be filled before painting, reinforced masonry paint will cover hairline cracks and crazing.

Painting exterior masonry

The outside walls of houses are painted for two main reasons: to give a bright, clean appearance, and to protect the surface from the weather. What you use as a finish and how you apply it depend on what the walls are made from, their condition, and the degree of protection they need. Bricks are traditionally left bare but may require a coat of paint if they've been painted before. Stuccoed walls are often painted to brighten the naturally dull, gray color of the cement; pebble-dashed surfaces may need a colorful coat to disguise unsightly patches. Or you may, of course, simply want to change the present color of your walls for a fresh appearance.

Working with a plan

Before you start painting outside masonry walls, plan your time carefully. Depending on the amount of preparation that is required, even a small house will take a few weeks to complete.

It is preferable, though, to tackle the whole job at once, since the weather may upset your timetable.

You can split the work into separate stages with days (or even weeks) in between, provided you divide the walls into manageable sections. Use window frames and doorframes, bays, and corners of walls to form break lines that will disguise joints.

Start at the top of the house, working from right to left, if you are right-handed.

● **Black dot denotes compatibility.** All surfaces must be clean, sound, dry, and free from organic growth.

FINISHES FOR MASONRY

	Cement paint	Exterior latex paint	Reinforced latex paint	Solvent-thinned masonry paint	Textured coating	Floor paint
SUITABLE TO COVER						
Brick	●	●	●	●	●	●
Stone	●	●	●	●	●	●
Concrete	●	●	●	●	●	●
Stucco	●	●	●	●	●	●
Exposed-aggregate concrete	●	●	●	●	●	●
Asbestos cement	●	●	●	●	●	●
Latex paint		●	●	●	●	●
Oil-based paint		●	●	●	●	●
Cement paint	●	●	●	●		●
DRYING TIME: HOURS						
Touch-dry	1–2	1–2	2–3	1–2	6	2–3
Recoatable	24	4	24	24	24–48	12–24
THINNERS: SOLVENTS						
Water-thinned	●	●	●		●	
Solvent-thinned				●		●
NUMBER OF COATS						
Normal conditions	2	2	1–2	2	1	1–2
COVERAGE: DEPENDING ON WALL TEXTURE						
Sq. ft. per quart		150–400	120–250	120–225		180–550
Sq. ft. per pound	30–75				20–40	
METHOD OF APPLICATION						
Brush	●	●	●	●	●	●
Roller	●	●	●	●	●	●
Spray gun	●	●	●	●		●

Techniques for painting masonry

1 Cut in with a gentle scrubbing motion

2 Protect downspouts with newspaper

3 Use a banister brush Tackle deeply textured wall surfaces with a banister brush.

Using the correct roller When painting heavy textures, use a roller that has a deep pile. Switch to a medium pile for light textures and smooth surfaces.

1 Spray onto the apex of outside corners

2 Spray inside corners as separate surfaces

Spray gun Rent a high-quality spray gun and a small portable compressor.

Using paintbrushes

Choose a brush that is 4 to 6 inches wide for painting walls; larger ones are heavy and tiring to use. A good-quality brush with coarse bristles will last longer on rough walls. For effective coverage, apply the paint with vertical strokes, crisscrossed with horizontal ones. You will find it necessary to stipple paint into textured surfaces.

Cutting in Painting up to features such as a door, window, and baseboard trim is known as cutting in. On a smooth surface, you should be able to paint a reasonably straight edge following the line of the trim—but it's difficult to apply the paint to a heavily textured wall with a normal brush stroke. Don't just apply more paint in the hope of overcoming the problem; instead, touch only the tip of the brush to the wall, using a gentle scrubbing action **(1)**, then brush out from the edge to spread excess paint once the texture is filled.

Wipe splashed paint from any trim with a cloth dampened with the appropriate thinner.

Painting behind downspouts To protect downspouts, tape a piece of newspaper around them. Stipple behind the downspout with a brush **(2)**, then move the newspaper down the pipe to mask the next section.

Painting with a banister brush Use a banister brush **(3)** to paint deep textures such as pebble dash. Pour some paint into a roller tray and dip the brush in to load the bristles. Scrub the paint onto the wall, using circular strokes to work it into the uneven surface.

Using a paint roller

A roller will apply paint three times as fast as a brush. Use a deep-pile roller for heavy textures, and one with a medium pile for lightly textured or smooth walls. Rollers wear out very quickly on rough walls, so have a spare sleeve handy. When painting with a roller, vary the angle of the stroke to ensure even coverage. Use a brush to cut into angles and obstructions.

A paint tray is difficult to use at the top of an extension ladder unless you install a support bracket.

Using a spray gun

Spraying is the quickest and most efficient way to apply paint to a large expanse of wall. But you will have to mask all the areas you don't want to paint, using newspaper and masking tape, and set drop cloths to prevent overspray.

Thin the paint by about 10 percent, and set the spray gun according to the manufacturer's instructions to suit the particular paint. Make sure to wear a respirator.

Hold the gun about 9 inches away from the wall and keep it moving with even, parallel passes. Slightly overlap each pass and try to keep the gun pointing directly at the surface. Trigger the gun just before each pass, and release it at the end of the stroke.

To cover a large blank wall evenly, spray it with vertical bands of paint, overlapping each band by about 4 inches.

Spray outside corners by aiming the gun directly at the apex so that paint falls evenly on both surfaces **(1)**. When two walls meet at an inside corner, spray each surface separately **(2)**.

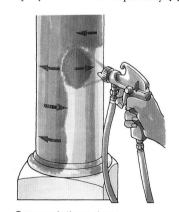
Spray-painting columns
Columns on porches and porticos should be painted in a series of overlapping vertical bands. Apply the bands by running the spray gun from side to side as you work down the column.

Treating painted masonry

Painted masonry inside the house is usually in fairly good condition, and apart from a good cleaning to remove dust and grease and a light sanding to give a key for the new finish, there is little else you need to do. Outside, however, it's a different matter. Exterior surfaces, subjected to extremes of heat, cold, and rain, are likely to be affected to some degree by stains, flaking, and chalkiness.

Curing a chalky surface

Rub the palm of your hand lightly over the surface of the wall to see if it is chalky. If the paint rubs off as a powdery deposit, treat the wall before you repaint.

Brush the surface with a stiff-bristle brush, then paint the whole wall liberally with a stabilizing primer, which will bind the chalky surface so that paint will adhere to it. Use a white stabilizing primer, which can also serve as an undercoat. Clean any splashes from surrounding woodwork with solvent.

If the wall is very dusty, apply a second coat of stabilizer after about 16 hours. Wait another 16 hours before applying paint.

A chalky surface needs stabilizing

Dealing with flaky paint

Poor surface preparation or incompatible paint and preparatory treatments are common causes of flaky paintwork. Damp walls will also cause flaking, so cure the damp and let the wall dry out before further treatment.

A new coat of paint will not bind to a flaky surface, so attend to this before you start painting. Use a paint scraper and a stiff-bristle brush to remove all loose material. Coarse sandpaper should finish the job, or at least feather the edges of any stubborn patches. Stabilize the surface as for chalky walls before repainting.

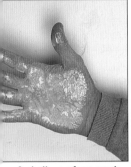

Strip flaky paintwork to a sound surface

Treating a stained chimney

If the outlines of brick courses show up as brown staining on a painted chimney, you can be sure it is caused by a breakdown of the internal flue liner of the chimney. Defective lining allows tar deposits to migrate through the mortar joints to the outer paintwork. To solve the problem, first repair the old flue liner or install a new one; then treat the brown stains with a stain-blocking primer/sealer before applying a fresh coat of paint.

Chimney stained by tar deposits from the flue

Stripping painted masonry

In the past, even sound brickwork was often painted, simply to brighten up a house. In some areas of the country where painted masonry is traditional, there is every reason to continue with the practice. Indeed, houses with soft, inferior brickwork were frequently painted when they were built in order to protect them from the weather—and to strip them now could have serious consequences. But if the brick on your house is in good condition and doesn't need paint to protect it, then removing the paint is an option—albeit an expensive one.

Restoring painted brickwork to its natural condition is not an easy task. It is generally a messy business involving the use of toxic materials that have to be handled with care and disposed of safely. Extensive scaffolding may be required, and most important, getting the masonry entirely clean demands considerable experience. For all these reasons, it is advisable to hire professionals to do the work for you.

To determine whether the outcome is likely to be successful, ask the company you are thinking of hiring to strip an inconspicuous patch of masonry, using the chemicals they recommend for the job. The results may indicate that it is better to repaint—in which case, choose a good-quality masonry paint that will let moisture within the walls evaporate.

A painted wall in need of restoration

Paths, driveways, and patios

For some people, installing any type of hardscaping (pathways, walls, driveways, and patios) is considered almost antithetical to the whole idea of gardening. They must envision a complete yard devoid of plants, trees, and grass. But for the rest of us, introducing hard elements like stone, brick, or concrete for a variety of uses not only makes our landscaping work better, it also creates a textured counterpoint to all the plantings that surround the hardscaping.

Paved patio
A patio area that's surrounded by stone or brick walls makes a perfect retreat.

Hardscape design

The marriage of different materials offers numerous possibilities. It may be convenient to define areas for walks or patios, but these are only names to describe the function of those particular areas. There's no reason why you cannot blend one area into another by using the same material throughout, or by employing similar colors to link one type of paving with another.

Having so many choices at your disposal does have its drawbacks: There's a strong temptation to experiment with any and every combination. But a few well-chosen materials that complement the house and its surroundings produce an effect that's far more appealing.

Sometimes, a hard and unyielding surface can be softened by the addition of foliage.

Working with concrete

Concrete is more versatile than some people think. It may appear to be a rather drab, utilitarian material for garden use, but you can add texture and color to ordinary concrete, or use one of the many types of cast concrete slabs and bricks made for paving patios, paths, and driveways.

Ingredients of concrete

Concrete in its simplest form consists of cement and fine particles of stone (sand and pebbles), known as aggregate. The dry ingredients are mixed with water to create a chemical reaction with the cement, which binds the aggregate into a hard, dense material.

The initial hardening process takes place quite quickly. The mix becomes unworkable after a couple of hours, depending on the temperature and humidity. But the concrete has no real strength for three to seven days.

The hardening process continues for up to a month, or as long as there is moisture still present within the concrete. Moisture is essential to the reaction. Consequently, concrete must not be allowed to dry out too quickly during the first few days.

Cement Standard portland cement, sold in 90-lb. bags, is used for on-site mixing of concrete. When dry, it is a fine gray powder.

Sand Sharp sand, a fairly coarse and gritty material, constitutes part of the aggregate of a concrete mix. Don't buy fine builder's sand used for mortar. And avoid unwashed or beach sand, both of which contain impurities that can affect the quality of the concrete.

Lumberyards and masonry supply outlets sell sharp sand by the cubic yard. For small jobs, it's also sold in large plastic bags that are easy to transport in a car.

Coarse aggregate This is gravel or crushed stone composed of stones ranging in size from about ¼ to ¾ inch for normal use. It's usually sold in bulk cubic yards, like sand, but is sometimes available in bags.

Pigments Special pigments can be added to a concrete mix to color it,

but it's difficult to guarantee an even color from one batch to another.

Combined aggregate In some areas, masonry supply outlets sell a combined aggregate (sometimes called ballast) that is a sand and gravel mix in the proper proportions for concrete use.

Dry-mix concrete You can buy dry cement—sand and aggregate mixed to the required proportions—for making concrete. Choose the proportion that best suits the job you have in mind. The dry ingredients for erecting fenceposts make up one typical ready-mixed product.

Concrete mix is sold in various-size bags up to 100 pounds. Available from the usual outlets, this is a more expensive way of buying concrete ingredients, but it's a simple and convenient method of ordering exactly the amount you need. Before you add water, make sure the ingredients are mixed thoroughly.

Water Use ordinary tap water. Impurities and salt contained in river or sea water are detrimental to concrete.

Admixtures Various additives (called admixtures) are available for concrete work. Air-entrainment is one that's frequently used during cold weather to avoid the damage done by freeze-and-thaw cycles. This is not something you can add to your concrete mix. It has to be done at a concrete plant.

Ready-mix concrete Ready-mix concrete is delivered by truck. You can stipulate the type of mix you want when ordering. There's usually a minimum order of at least a couple of cubic yards. But sometimes a truck will have a small amount left from a previous order and will drop it off at your job on the way back to the concrete plant.

Rent a small mixing machine if you have to prepare a large volume of concrete, but for most jobs it's more convenient to mix it by hand. It isn't necessary to weigh the ingredients—simply mix them by volume, choosing the proportions that suit the job at hand.

Mixing by hand

Use two large buckets to measure the ingredients, one for the cement and (in order to keep the cement perfectly dry) another identical bucket for the sand and coarse aggregate. Using two shovels is also a good idea.

Measure the materials accurately, leveling them with the rim of the bucket. Tap the side of the bucket with the shovel as you load it with sand or cement so that the loose particles are shaken down.

Mix the sand and aggregate first, on a hard, flat surface. Scoop a depression in the pile for the cement and mix all the ingredients until the mixture is an even color.

Form another depression and add some water. Push the dry ingredients into the water from around the edge until the surface water has been absorbed, then mix the batch by chopping the concrete with the shovel **(1)**. Add more water, then turn the concrete from the bottom of the pile and chop it as before until the whole batch has an even consistency.

To test the workability of the mix, form a series of ridges by dragging the blade of the shovel across the pile **(2)**. The surface of the concrete should be flat and even in texture, and the ridges should hold their shape without slumping.

Mixing by machine

Make sure you set the concrete mixer on a hard, level surface and that the drum is upright before you start the motor. Use a bucket to pour half the required coarse aggregate into the drum and add water. Add the sand and cement

1 Mixing ingredients
Mix the ingredients by chopping the concrete mix with the shovel. Turn the mix over and chop again.

2 Testing the mix
Make ridges with the back of the shovel to test the workability of the mix.

alternately in small batches, plus the rest of the aggregate. Keep on adding water little by little along with the other ingredients.

Let the batch mix for a few minutes. Then tilt the drum of the mixer while it is still rotating and turn out some of the concrete into a wheelbarrow so you can test its consistency (see above). If necessary, return the concrete to the mixer to adjust it.

Storing materials

If you buy sand and aggregate in sacks, use as much as you need for the job and keep the rest bagged until the next use. Pile loose ingredients separately on a hard surface or thick polyethylene sheets. Cover the piles with weighted sheets of plastic.

Cement is usually sold in paper sacks, which will absorb moisture from the ground, so pile them on a board., preferably in a dry shed or garage. If you have to store it outdoors, cover the bags with plastic sheets weighted with bricks.

Once a bag is opened, cement will absorb moisture from the air, so keep a partly used bag sealed in a plastic bag.

If you need a lot of concrete for a driveway or large patio, it may be worth ordering a delivery of ready-mixed concrete from a local supplier. Always contact the supplier well in advance to discuss your particular requirements. Specify the proportions of the ingredients and say whether you require a retarding agent to slow down the setting time. (Once a normal mix of concrete is delivered, you will have about 2 hours in which to finish the job. A retarding agent can add a couple of hours to the setting time.) Tell the supplier exactly what you need the concrete for, and accept his advice. For quantities of less than 8 cubic yards, you may have to shop around for a supplier who is willing to deliver without tacking on an additional charge.

In order to avoid moving the concrete too far by wheelbarrow, you will want it discharged as close to the site as possible, if not directly into place. However, the chute on a delivery truck can reach only so far, and if the vehicle is too large or heavy to drive onto your property, you will need several helpers to move the concrete while it is still workable. A single cubic yard of concrete will fill 25 to 30 wheelbarrows. If it takes longer than 30 to 40 minutes to discharge the load, you may have to pay extra.

Professional mixing

Some companies deliver concrete ingredients and mix them to your specifications on the spot. You have to move the concrete in a wheelbarrow and pour it into place. This is a good option if you don't know exactly how much concrete you need.

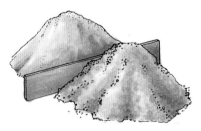

Storing sand and aggregate
Piles of sand and aggregate with dividing board

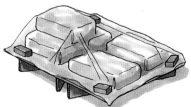

Storing cement
Raise bags of cement off the ground and cover them with plastic sheeting.

Designing concrete paving

Designing simple concrete pads may not be very complicated, but there are important factors to consider if the concrete is to be durable. At the least, you will have to decide on the thickness of the concrete that is needed to support the weight of traffic, and the surface slope required to drain off water.

When the area of concrete is large, or an irregular shape, you need to incorporate control joints to allow the material to expand and contract. If a pad is for a habitable building, it must include a vapor barrier to exclude moisture rising from the ground. Even the proportions of sand, cement, and aggregate in the mix have to be considered carefully.

• Sloping floors
Although you can build upon a perfectly flat base, it is a good idea to slope the floor toward the door of a garage or outbuilding that is to be scrubbed out from time to time. Alternatively, slope a floor in two directions toward the middle to form a shallow drain that runs to the door.

Deciding on the slope

A freestanding pad can be laid perfectly level, especially to support a small outbuilding. But a very slight slope or fall will prevent water from collecting in puddles if you have failed to get the concrete absolutely flat. If a pad is laid directly against a house, it must have a definite fall away from the building, and any parking area or driveway must shed water to provide adequate traction for vehicles and to minimize the formation of ice.

USE OF PAVING	ANGLE OF FALL
Pathways	Not required
Driveways	1 inch per yard
Patios Parking spaces	1 inch per yard
Pads for garages and outbuilding	½ inch per yard

Recommended thicknesses for concrete

The normal thicknesses recommended for concrete paving assume it will be laid on a firm subsoil. If the soil is clay or peat, increase the thickness by about 50 percent. The same applies to a new site, where the soil may not be compacted. Unless the concrete is for pedestrian traffic only, lay a subbase of compacted gravel below the paving. This will absorb ground movement without affecting the concrete itself. A subbase is not essential for a very lightweight structure, such as a small wood shed or for a modest-size patio.

Pathways
For pedestrian traffic only:
Concrete: 3 inches
Subbase: Not required

Patios
Any extensive area of concrete for pedestrian traffic:
Concrete: 4 inches
Subbase: 4 inches

Driveways
Drive used for an average family car only:
Concrete: 5 inches
Subbase: 6 inches

For heavier vehicles, such as delivery trucks:
Concrete: 6 inches
Subbase: 6 inches

Light structures
Support pad for a woodshed:
Concrete: 3 inches
Subbase: 3 inches.

Parking spaces
Exposed paving for parking family car:
Concrete: 5 inches
Subbase: 6 inches

Garages
Thicken up the edges of a garage pad to support the weight of the walls:
Concrete:
Floor: 5 inches
Edges: 8 inches
Subbase: minimum 6 inches

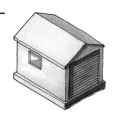

Allowing for expansion

Changes in temperature cause concrete to expand and contract. If this movement is allowed to happen at random, a pad or pathway will crack at the weakest point.

Control joints made of a compressible material will either absorb the movement or concentrate the force in predetermined areas where it will do little harm. The joints should meet the sides of a concrete area at more-or-less 90 degrees. Always place a control joint between concrete and a wall.

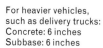

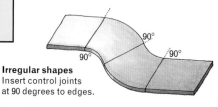

Irregular shapes
Insert control joints at 90 degrees to edges.

Positioning control joints The exact position will depend on the area and shape of the concrete.

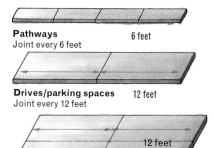

Pathways   6 feet
Joint every 6 feet

Drives/parking spaces   12 feet
Joint every 12 feet

       12 feet

Concrete pads
Joints no more than 12 feet apart and around any floor drains

Divide a pad into equal bays if:
• The length is more than twice the width.
• The longest dimension is more than 40 times the thickness.
• The longest dimension exceeds 12 feet

Keep the shovel as clean as possible between mixing batches of concrete, and at the end of a working day wash all traces of concrete from your tools and wheelbarrow. When you have finished using a concrete mixer, add a few shovels of coarse aggregate and a little water, then run the machine for a couple of minutes to scour the inside of the drum. Dump the aggregate, then hose out the drum with clean water. Shovel unused concrete into sacks, ready for disposal at a refuse dump, and wash the mixing area with a stiff broom. Never hose concrete or any separate ingredient into a drain.

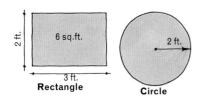

CALCULATING AREAS

Squares and rectangles
Calculate the area of rectangular paving by multiplying width by length.

Example:
2 ft. x 3 ft. = 6 sq. ft.
78 in. x 117 in. = 9126 sq. in. or 7 sq. yd.

Circles
Use the formula πr^2 to calculate the area of a circle (π = 3.14, r = radius of circle).

Example:
$3.14 \times 2 \text{ ft.}^2 = 3.14 \times 4 = 12.56$ sq. ft.
$3.14 \times 78 \text{ in.}^2 = 3.14 \times 6084 = 19,104$ sq. in. or 14.75 sq. yd.

Rectangle — 6 sq.ft. (2 ft. x 3 ft.)
Circle — 2 ft.

Irregular shapes

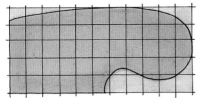

Square up an irregular shape to calculate area

To estimate the amount of materials that will be required, you need to calculate the volume of concrete in the finished pad, path, or drive. Measure the surface area of the site and multiply that figure by the thickness of the concrete.

Estimating quantities of concrete
Use the grid diagram to estimate the volume of concrete you will need by reading off the area of the site in square yards and tracing it horizontally to meet the angled line indicating concrete thickness. Trace the line up to find the volume in cubic yards.

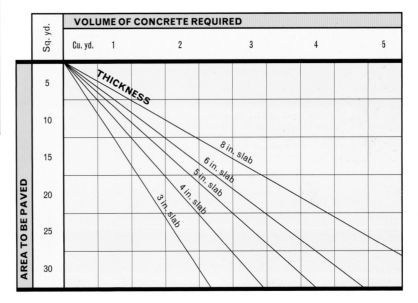

Estimating quantities of ingredients
Use the bar charts below to estimate the quantities of cement, sand, and aggregate you will require to mix up the volume of concrete arrived at by using the chart above.

The figures are based on the quantity of ingredients required to mix 1 cubic yard of concrete for a particular type of mix, plus about 10 percent to allow for waste.

	CUBIC YARDS OF CONCRETE	1.00	1.50	2.00	2.50	3.00	3.50	4.00	4.50	5.00
GENERAL-PURPOSE MIX										
	Cement (94-lb. bag)	7.00	10.50	14.00	17.50	21.00	24.50	28.00	31.50	35.00
plus	Sand (cubic yard)	0.50	0.75	1.00	1.25	1.50	1.75	2.00	2.25	2.50
	Aggregate (cubic yard)	0.75	1.15	1.50	1.90	2.25	2.65	3.00	3.40	3.75
or	Ballast (cubic yard)	0.90	1.35	1.80	2.25	2.70	3.15	3.60	4.05	4.50
FOUNDATION MIX										
	Cement (94-lb. bag)	6.00	9.00	12.00	15.00	18.00	21.00	24.00	27.00	30.00
plus	Sand (cubic yard)	0.55	0.80	1.10	1.40	1.65	1.95	2.20	2.50	2.75
	Aggregate (cubic yard)	0.75	1.15	1.50	1.90	2.25	2.65	3.00	3.40	3.75
or	Ballast (cubic yard)	1.00	1.50	2.00	2.50	3.00	3.50	4.00	4.50	5.00
PAVING MIX										
	Cement (94-lb. bag)	9.00	13.50	18.00	22.50	27.00	31.50	36.00	40.50	45.00
plus	Sand (cubic yard)	0.45	0.70	0.90	1.15	1.35	1.60	1.80	2.00	2.25
	Aggregate (cubic yard)	0.75	1.15	1.50	1.90	2.25	2.65	3.00	3.40	3.75
or	Ballast (cubic yard)	1.00	1.50	2.00	2.50	3.00	3.50	4.00	4.50	5.00

Installing a concrete pad

Installing a simple pad as a base for a small shed or similar structure involves all the basic principles of concrete work including building a retaining formwork and pouring, leveling, and finishing the surface. If the base is less than 6 feet square, there's no need to include control joints.

Mixing concrete by volume

Whatever container you use to measure out the ingredients (shovel, bucket, or wheelbarrow), the proportions remain the same.

MIXING CONCRETE BY VOLUME			
Type of mix	Proportions		For 1 cu.yd. concrete
GENERAL PURPOSE			
Use in most situations including covered pads other than garage floors	plus	1 part cement	7 bags (94 lb. each)
		2 parts sand	0.5 cu. yd.
		3 parts aggregate	0.7 cu. yd.
	or	4 parts ballast	0.9 cu. yd.
FOUNDATION			
Use for footings at the base of masonry walls	plus	1 part cement	6 bags (94 lb. each)
		2½ parts sand	0.5 cu. yd.
		3½ parts aggregate	0.7 cu. yd.
	or	5 parts ballast	1.0 cu. yd.
PAVING			
Use for parking areas, drives, footpaths, and garage floors	plus	1 part cement	9 bags (94 lb. each)
		1½ parts sand	0.4 cu. yd.
		2½ parts aggregate	0.7 cu. yd.
	or	3½ parts ballast	1.0 cu. yd.

Excavating the site

First, mark out the area of the pad with string lines attached to pegs driven into the ground outside the work area **(1)**. Remove the lines to excavate the site, but replace them afterward to help position the forms that will hold the concrete in place.

Remove the topsoil and vegetation within the site down to a level that allows for the combined thickness of concrete and subbase. Extend the area of excavation about 6 inches outside the space allowed for the pad. Cut back any roots you find, and if there's any turf, put it aside to cover the backfill surrounding the completed pad. Finally, level the bottom of the excavation by dragging a board across it **(2)** and compact the soil with a lawn roller or plate compactor.

Erecting the formwork

Until the concrete sets hard, it must be supported all round by forms. For a straightforward rectangular slab, construct the forms from standard ¾-inch-thick lumber. The planks, which must be as wide as the finished depth of concrete, need to be held in place temporarily with 2 x 2-inch wood stakes. Scrap lumber, as long as it's straight, works well for forms. If you have to join boards, butt them end to end, nailing a cleat on the outside **(3)**.

Using the string lines as a guide, erect one board at the high end of the slab and drive stakes behind it at about 3-foot intervals or less, with one for each corner. The tops of the stakes and board must be level and need to correspond exactly to the proposed surface of the slab. Nail the board to the stakes **(4)**.

Set up another board opposite the first one, but before you nail it to the stakes, check it for level with the first board using a level and a straightedge. Work out the difference in level from one side of the pad to the other. For example, a pad that is about 8 feet wide should drop about 1 inch over that distance. Tape a shim of scrap wood to one end of the straightedge and, with the shim resting on the low stakes, place the other end on the opposite board **(5)**. Drive down each low stake until the spirit level reads horizontal, and then nail the board flush with the tops of the stakes.

Erect the ends of the form. Allowing the boards to overshoot at the corners will make it easier to dismantle them when the concrete has set **(6)**. Use the straightedge, without the shim, to level the boards from end to end.

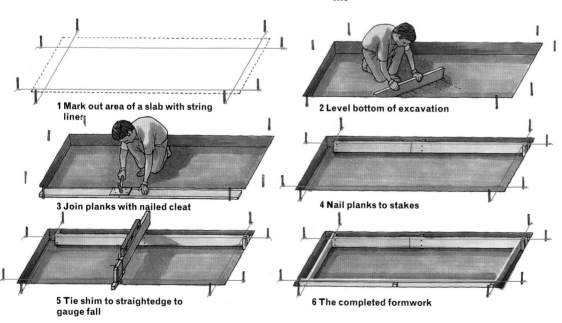

1 Mark out area of a slab with string lines

2 Level bottom of excavation

3 Join planks with nailed cleat

4 Nail planks to stakes

5 Tie shim to straightedge to gauge fall

6 The completed formwork

Completing the pad

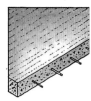

If you want to enlarge your patio, simply butt a new section of concrete against the existing pad. The butt joint will in itself serve as a control joint.
To add a narrow strip to a pad (so that you can erect a larger shed, for example), drill holes in the edge of the pad and use epoxy adhesive to glue in short lengths of rebar before pouring the fresh concrete.

Laying the subbase
Bank run gravel, a natural mixture of gravel and sand, is an ideal material for a subbase. But you can use crushed stone or screened gravel too. Be sure to remove any scrap building materials and vegetation from the subbase material. Then level its surface and compact it with a roller or a tamper made from a 4 x 4 with a wood pad nailed to the bottom **(7)**. If there are any stubborn lumps, break them up with a heavy hammer. Fill in low spots with more subbase material until the subbase reaches the underside of the form boards.

Filling with concrete
Mix the concrete as near to the site as you can and transport the fresh mix to the form in a wheelbarrow. Set up a firm runway using scaffolding boards if the ground is soft, especially around the forms' perimeter.

Dampen the subbase and formwork with a fine spray, and let surface water evaporate before tipping the concrete in place. Start filling from one end of the site and push the concrete firmly into the corners **(8)**. Rake it level until the concrete stands about ¾ inch above the level of the boards.

Tamp down the concrete with the edge of a 2-inch-thick plank that is long enough to reach across the forms. Starting at one end of the site, compact the concrete with steady blows of the plank, moving it along by a couple of inches each time **(9)**. Cover the whole area twice and then remove excess concrete, using the plank with a sawing action **(10)**. Fill any low spots, then compact and level the concrete once more.

To retain the moisture, cover the pad with sheets of polyethylene, taped at the joints and held down with bricks around the edge **(11)**. Try to avoid laying concrete in very cold weather. But if that's unavoidable, use ready-mix concrete treated to resist freezing for the job.

It's perfectly safe to walk on the concrete after three days, but leave it for about a week before removing the forms and erecting a shed or similar outbuilding.

Finishing the edges
If any of the edges are exposed, the sharp corners could cause a painful injury. Use an edging float to smooth and round the edges.

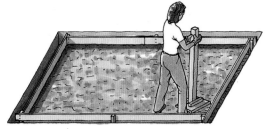

7 Level subbase with lawn roller or tamper tool

8 Pour concrete, starting in one corner

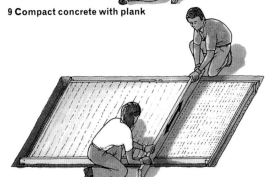

9 Compact concrete with plank

10 Use sawing action to remove excess concrete

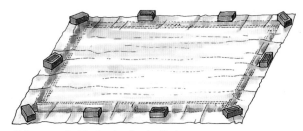

11 Cover pad with sheets of polyethylene

Walks and driveways

Walks and drives are laid and compacted in the same way as rectangular pads, using similar forms to contain the concrete. However, the shape of most walks and drives makes the inclusion of control joints essential to allow for expansion and contraction. You will have to install a subbase under a driveway, but a footpath can be laid on compacted soil leveled with sand. Establish a slight fall across the site to shed rain.

Laying out paths and drives

Excavate the site, allowing for the thickness of the subbase and concrete. Level the bottom of the excavation as accurately as you can, using a board to scrape the surface flat.

Drive accurately leveled pegs into the ground along the site to act as reference points for the form boards. Space them about 6 feet apart along the center of the walk. Drive in the first peg until its top corresponds exactly to the proposed surface of the concrete. Use either a long straightedge and a level or a water level to position every other peg.

To make a water level, push a short length of transparent plastic tubing into each end of a garden hose. Holding both ends together, fill the hose with water until it appears in the tube at both ends. Then mark the level on both tubes. As long as the ends remain open, the water level at each end is constant, enabling you to establish a level over any distance, even around obstacles or corners. When you move the hose, plug both ends to retain the water.

Tie one end of the hose to the first reference peg, ensuring that the marked level aligns with the top of the peg. Use the other end to establish the level of every other peg along the pathway **(1)**.

To set a fall with a water level, make a mark on one tube below the surface of the water and use that as a gauge for the top of the peg.

Erecting formwork

Construct forms from ¾-inch-thick boards and 2 x 2 stakes. To check for level, rest a straightedge on the nearest reference peg **(2)**.

If the driveway or walk is very long, wood forms can be expensive. It may be cheaper to rent metal forms. Standard forms are made from rigid units, but flexible sections are available to form curves.

To bend wood forms, make a series of closely spaced parallel saw cuts across the width of the plank in the area of the curve **(3)**. The board is less likely to break if you place the saw cuts on the inside of the bend.

It's usually about ½ inch thick. Cut each expansion strip to fit exactly between the formwork and to match the depth of the concrete. Before pouring, hold the control joints in place with mounds of concrete and nails driven into the formwork on each side of the strip **(4)**. As you fill the formwork, pack more concrete on both sides of each joint and tamp toward the strip from both sides so that it is not dislodged.

On a narrow path, to prevent the concrete from cracking between joints, cut ¾-inch-deep grooves across the concrete to form dummy joints alternating with the physical ones. The simplest method is to cut a length of T-section steel to fit between the form boards. Place the strip on the surface of the wet concrete and tap it down with a mallet **(5)**. Carefully lift the strip out of the concrete to leave a neat impression. If the concrete moves after it's dry, a crack will develop unnoticed at the bottom of the groove. Install expansion material between the concrete and an adjoining wall, or other obstructions, to absorb expansion.

1 A water level made from garden hose

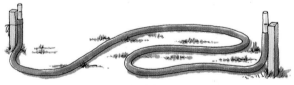

2 Level form using reference pegs

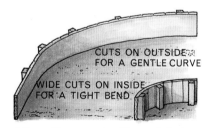

3 Curved forms made with wood planks

Installing control joints

Install a permanent expansion joint every 6 to 8 feet for a walk, and every 13 or 14 feet along a driveway. For a patio, you can install similar joints or use alternate-bay construction (see facing page).

Expansion-joint material is available at masonry supply outlets.

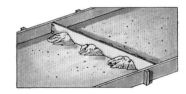

4 Expansion strip with concrete and nails

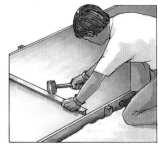

5 Make dummy joint with T-shaped steel

Alternate-bay method of construction

It is not always possible to pour all the concrete in a single operation. In such cases, it's easier to divide the form in half with additional planks to create two separate bays.

By filling alternate bays with concrete, you have plenty of time to finish each section and more room in which to maneuver. It is a convenient way to lay a large patio—which would be practically impossible to pour and finish in one go—and it is the only method you can use for driveways or walks that butt against a wall. Alternate-bay construction is also frequently used for building a driveway on a steep slope to prevent the heavy, wet concrete from slumping downhill.

There is no need to install control joints when using bay construction, but you may want to form dummy joints for a neat appearance (see facing page).

Laying concrete next to a wall

Stand in the empty bays so you can pour and smooth the concrete against the wall. When the first bays have set hard, remove the intermediate form boards and fill the gaps. Trowel the surface level with the set concrete. Don't use a vehicle on a concrete driveway for 10 days after pouring.

Finishing concrete bays next to wall

Surface finishes

The surface finish produced by striking off concrete with a plain screed board is adequate for a workmanlike foundation slab, walk, or driveway. But you can produce a range of other finishes using simple hand tools and basic skills.

Create smooth finish with wooden float

Float finishes

You can smooth the poured concrete by sweeping a wooden float across the surface, or make an even finer texture by finishing with a steel float. Let the concrete dry out a little before using a float, or you will bring water to the top and weaken it, which will eventually result in a dusty residue on the hardened concrete. Bridge the formwork with a thick plank so that you can reach the center, or rent a steel float with a long handle for large slabs.

Brush-finished concrete

Brush finishes

To produce a finely textured surface, draw a yard broom across the setting concrete. Finish the concrete initially with a wooden float and then make parallel passes with the broom, held at a low angle to avoid tearing the surface.

Texture surface with broom

Exposed aggregate finish

Embedding small stones or pebbles in the surface makes a very attractive and practical finish, although you will need a little practice in order to do it successfully.

1 Tamp pebbles into fresh concrete

2 Wash cement from around the pebbles

Scatter dampened pebbles onto the freshly laid concrete and embed them firmly with a short board until they are flush with the surface **(1)**. Place a plank across the forms and apply your full weight to make sure the surface is even. Let the floor harden for a while until all the surface water has evaporated, then use a very fine spray and a brush to wash away the cement from around the pebbles until they protrude **(2)**. Cover the concrete for about 24 hours, then lightly wash the surface again to clean any sediment off the pebbles. Cover the concrete again and let it harden thoroughly.

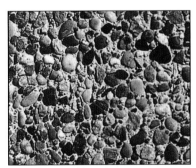
Exposed aggregate finish

Paving slabs

Shapes and sizes

If your only experience of paving slabs is the rather bland variety used for many public walkways and courtyards, then cast concrete paving may not seem like an attractive option for the landscaping around your house. But it pays to look around. There's a wide variety of residential pavers in many different shapes and colors.

Colors and textures

Paving slabs are made by hydraulic pressing or casting in molds to create the desired surface finish. Pigments and selected aggregates added to the concrete mix are used to create the illusion of a range of muted colors or natural stone. Combining two or more colors or textures within the same area of paving can be very striking.

Regular or informal paving
Constructing a simple grid from square slabs (left) is relatively easy. Though more difficult to lay, mixed paving (below) is richer in texture, color, and shape.

Paving slabs come in a fairly standard range of shapes and modular sizes. It is possible to carry the largest slabs without help, but get an assistant to help maneuver them into place.

Square and rectangular
A single size and shape can be employed to make gridlike patterns or, when staggered, to create a bonded brick effect. Use rectangular slabs to form a basket-weave or herringbone pattern. Or combine different sizes to create the impression of random paving, or mix slabs with a different type of paving to create a colorful contrast.

Regular grid

Staggered

**Basket-weave
pattern**

Herringbone pattern   **Random paving**

Hexagonal
Hexagonal slabs form honeycomb patterns. Use half-slabs to edge areas that are paved in straight lines.

Hexagonal slab

Honeycomb pattern

Half-hexagonal slabs

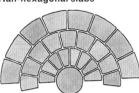

Tapered slabs
Use tapered slabs to edge ponds and for encircling trees or making curved steps. Progressively larger slabs can be used for laying circular areas of paving.

Circular slabs
Circular slabs make perfect individual stepping-stones across a lawn or flowerbed, but for a wide area, fill the spaces between with stones or gravel.

**Butted
circular slabs**

Laying paving

Laying paving slabs involves a good deal of physical labor, but in terms of technique it's no more complicated than tiling a wall. Accurate planning and careful placement, especially during the early stages, will help you achieve top-notch results.

Laying out the area of paving

Wherever practical, plan an area of paving so that it can be laid with whole slabs only. This eliminates the time-consuming task of cutting units to fit. Use pegs and string to mark out the perimeter of the paved area, and check the measurements before you excavate.

You can use a straight wall as a reference line and measure away from it. If possible, leave a 4- to 6-inch margin of gravel between the paving and wall. A gravel margin not only saves time and money by using fewer slabs but also provides an area for planting climbers and for adequate drainage to keep the wall dry.

Establish a slope of ⅛ inch per yard across the paving so that most of the surface water will drain into the surrounding yard. If the paving area is bounded by structures on all four sides, you should install a drain before laying the pavers.

Because paving slabs are made to fairly precise dimensions, marking out an area simply involves accurate measurement, allowing for a ¼- to ⅜-inch gap between the slabs.

1 Tapered joint

Some slabs have sloping edges to provide a tapered joint **(1)**. These pavers should be butted edge to edge.

Preparing a base for paving

Paving slabs must be laid upon a firm, level base, but the depth and substance of that base depends on the type of soil and the proposed use of the paving.

For straightforward patios and walks, remove vegetation and top-soil to allow for the thickness of the slabs, plus a 1½-inch layer of sharp sand, and an extra ¾ inch so the paving will be below the level of surrounding turf in order to prevent damage to your lawn mower. Compact the soil with a garden roller and then spread the sand with a rake and level it by scraping and tamping with a length of 2 x 6 **(2)**.

To support heavier loads, or if the soil is composed of clay or peat,

2 Level sand base

lay a subbase of firmly compacted gravel or crushed stone to a depth of 3 or 4 inches before spreading the sand to level the surface. If you plan to park vehicles on the paving, increase the depth of the gravel or stone to about 6 inches.

Laying the paving slabs

Set up string lines again as a guide and lay the edging slabs on the sand, working in both directions from a corner. When you are satisfied with their positions, lift the slabs one at a time so you can set them on a bed of firm mortar (1 part cement to 4 parts sand). Lay a fist-size spot under each corner and one more to support the center of the slab **(3)**. If you intend to drive vehicles across the slabs, lay a continuous bed of mortar about 2 inches thick.

Lay three slabs at a time, inserting wooden spacers between them. Level each slab by tapping with a hammer and a block of wood to protect the surface **(4)**. Check the alignment.

Gauge the slope across the paving by setting up reference pegs along the high side. Drive them into the ground until the top of each corresponds to the finished surface of the paving, and then use a straightedge with a wood block tacked to one end to check the fall on the slabs **(5)**. Lay the remainder keeping the joints square. Remove the spacers before the mortar sets.

3 Lay spots of mortar

4 Level slabs

5 Check fall with level

Filling the joints

Don't walk on the paving for two to three days, until the mortar has set. If you have to cross the area, lay planks across the slabs to spread the load.

To fill the gaps between the slabs, brush a dry mortar mix of 1 part cement to 3 parts sand into the open joints **(6)**. Remove any surplus material from the paving surface, then sprinkle the area with a very fine spray of water to consolidate the mortar. Avoid dry-mortaring if rain is forecast. It can wash out the mortar.

Cutting paving slabs
To trim concrete paving slabs to size, start by marking a line across a slab with chalk or a soft pencil. Place the slab on a bed of sand and, using a cold chisel and hammer, chisel a groove about 1/8 inch deep along the line. When cutting a thick slab, continue the groove down both of the edges and across the underside.

Turn the slab facedown and, with the hammer, tap firmly along the groove until the slab splits. If need be, clean up the edge with the cold chisel.

When cutting slabs, always protect your eyes by wearing plastic goggles. Wear a face mask, too, if you use a circular saw or an angle grinder, as these throw up a great deal of dust.

6 Fill joints

Laying fieldstone paving

Informal walks and patios laid with irregular-shaped paving stones have always been popular. The random effect, which many find more appealing than the geometry of neatly laid slabs, is also easy to achieve.

Materials for crazing paving

You can use broken flat stones like slate or bluestone if you are able to find enough. These stones are quarried into flat sections and then cut into pieces with square edges. Randomly broken flat stones can be obtained at a very reasonable price if you collect them yourself. Select stones about 1½ to 2 inches thick, in a variety of shapes, colors, and sizes.

Walkway made of broken pieces of flat stone

Laying a base

You can set out string lines to define straight edges for stone paving, although edges will never be as precise as those made with regular cast concrete slabs.

You can also allow the stones to form an irregular junction with grass, perhaps setting one or two stones out from the edge. Lay a bed of sharp sand for the stones, as described for laying paving slabs.

Create an irregular edge to stone paving.

Laying the stones

Arrange an area of fieldstones (sometimes called flagstones), selecting them for a close fit but avoiding too many straight, continuous joints. Use a cold chisel and hammer to trim those that don't quite fit. Reserve larger stones for the perimeter. Small stones tend to break away.

Use a mallet or a block of wood and a hammer to bed each stone into the sand (1) until they are all perfectly stable and reasonably level. Having bedded an area approximately 1 square yard, use a straightedge and level to check the stones (2). If necessary, add or remove sand beneath individual stones until the area is level. When the main area is complete, fill in the larger gaps with small stones, tapping them into place with a mallet (3).

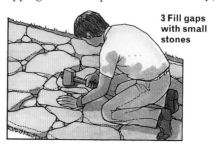

3 Fill gaps with small stones

Fill the joints by spreading more sand across the surface and sweeping it into the joints from all sides (4). You can also mix up a stiff, almost dry, mortar and press it into the joints with a trowel, leaving no gaps. Use an old paintbrush to smooth the mortared joints, then wipe the stones clean.

Laying stepping-stones

Place individual stones across a lawn to form a row of stepping-stones. Cut around the edge of each stone with a spade or trowel and remove the area of turf directly beneath. Scoop out the soil to allow for a 1-inch bed of sharp sand plus the stone, which must be about ¾ inch below the level of the surrounding turf. Tap the stone into the sand until it no longer rocks when you step on it.

Cut around stepping-stone with trowel

1 Bed stones in sand base

2 Check level across several stones

4 Sweep dry sand into joints

Stepping-stones form a garden walkway

Brick patterns

Paving with bricks

Unlike brick walls, which must be bonded in a certain way for stability, brick paths, patios, and car-parking areas can be laid to any pattern that appeals to you. Try out your ideas on graph paper, using the examples shown below for inspiration.

Concrete bricks, which have one finished surface, are often chamfered all round to define their shape and emphasize whatever pattern you choose. Many bricks have spacers molded into the sides to help form accurate joints. House bricks can be laid on edge or facedown, showing the wide face normally unseen in a wall.

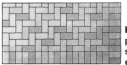

Herringbone pattern with straight edging

Angled herringbone with straight edging

Whole bricks surrounding colored half-bats

Staggered basket-weave pattern

Stretcher bond pattern

Cane weave pattern

Bricks make charming paths and walkways. The wide variety of textures and colors offers nearly endless pattern possibilities. But choose the type of brick carefully, keeping in mind the sort of use your paving will have to serve.

Brick paving

Ordinary house bricks are often used for paths and small patios, even though there is the risk of spalling in freezing conditions—unless they happen to be engineering bricks. Slightly uneven texture and color are the two big reasons why secondhand bricks (from demolition sites) are in demand for paving projects.

House bricks are not really suitable if the paved area is a parking space or driveway, especially one used by heavy vehicles. For a surface that will be durable under these severe conditions, use concrete bricks instead. These are generally slightly smaller than standard house bricks. In fact, there are many variations in shape, size, and color, making possible a wide range of approaches.

Providing a base for brick paving

Lay brick walkways and patios on a 3-inch-thick gravel base, covered with a 2-inch layer of compacted, slightly damp sharp sand. When laying concrete bricks for a drive, you need to increase the depth of the gravel to 6 inches. Fully compact the gravel so that sand from the bedding course is not lost to the subbase.

Provide a slope (for water runoff) on patios and drives, as described earlier for concrete. In cold climates this slope is especially important. If the water pools, it can freeze into a sheet of ice.

Retaining edges

Unless the brick path is laid against a wall or some similar structure, the edges of the paving must be

contained by a permanent restraint. Lumber treated with chemical preservative is one solution, constructed like the formwork for concrete. The edging boards should be flush with the surface of the path, but drive the stakes below ground so that they can be covered by soil or turf **(1)**.

Concrete paving, in particular, needs a more substantial edging of bricks set in concrete **(2)**. Dig a trench that is deep and wide enough to take a row of bricks on end plus a concrete foundation. Lay the bricks while the concrete is still wet. Hold them in place temporarily with a staked board while you pack more concrete behind the edging. Once the concrete has set, remove the board and lay gravel and sand in the excavation.

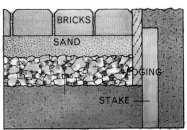

1 Wood retaining edge

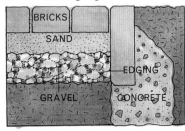

2 Brick retaining edge

Brick pavers
Pavers are available in a variety of colors, styles, and shapes. Textured units are ideal for nonslip garden walkways (above left). Mottled bricks make functional and eye-catching driveways and parking areas (below).

Laying the bricks

Plate compactor
Use a gas-powered, vibrating-plate compactor to prepare the subbase and embed the pavers.

Having chosen your bricks, prepared the ground, and set retaining edges, you can start laying your paving. Laying bricks over a wide area can be time consuming, so it helps if at least two people can work together, dividing up the various tasks between them. Also, it's well worth the extra expense of renting tools that will make the work faster and more efficient.

Compacting and leveling the sand

When the bricks are first laid on the sand they should project ⅜ inch above the edging restraints to allow for bedding them into the base later **(1)**.

Spread sand to about two-thirds of its finished thickness across the area to be paved and then compact it, using a rented plate compactor (above left).

Spread more sand on top and level it with a notched board that spans the edging **(2)**. If the area is too wide for a single board, lay leveling guides on the gravel base and scrape the sand to the required depth using a straightedge **(3)**. Then remove the guides and fill the voids carefully with sand

tightly. Fill any of the remaining spaces with bricks cut with a cold chisel and hammer. If you have a lot of cuts to make, consider renting a hydraulic brick cutter (bottom, far left). It cuts bricks quickly and cleanly.

When the area of paving is complete, run the vibrating plate over the surface two or three times until it has worked the bricks down into the sand flush with the outer edging **(5)**.

Vibrating the bricks will work some sand up between them; complete the job by brushing more kiln-dried, joint-filling sand across the finished paving and vibrating it into the open joints.

1 Start by laying bricks 3/8 inch above edging

2 Level sand with notched board   **3 For wide areas use guide boards**

4 Lay bricks in your chosen pattern

Hydraulic brick cutter

Bedding in the bricks

Lay the bricks on the sand in your chosen pattern. Start at one end of the site, kneeling on a board placed across the bricks **(4)**. Never stand on the bed of sand. Lay whole bricks only, leaving any gaps at the edges to be filled with cut bricks after you have laid an area of approximately 2 square yards. Butt the bricks together

5 A plate compactor levels and embeds bricks

A large patio or parking space may have to accommodate an existing drain cover, which often spoils the job's appearance. The solution is to replace the cover with a hollow access cover designed to be filled with pavers. To drain a large, flat area of paving, you can install a linear drainage channel that will carry water to the storm sewer.

Access cover

The metal frame of an access cover should be embedded in concrete, which is then covered with pavers that run up to the rim of the access hole. Make sure the rim is just below the finished paving surface.

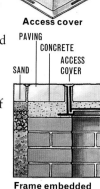

Access cover

Frame embedded in concrete

Drainage channel

Plastic U-shaped linear drainage channels, linked end to end, are embedded in a 4-inch-thick concrete base, which holds the channel in place. The first row of bricks on each side of the channel is embedded

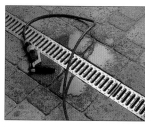

in the concrete, and should finish ⅛ to ¼ inch above the level of the plastic or metal grating used to cover the channel. You can cut the channel to length with a handsaw.

A special endcap is available for connecting to a main sewer, or you can drain the water into a dry well about 4 feet square and at least 4 feet deep. Fill the dry well with coarse gravel or crushed stone.

Wood pathways

Cobblestones and gravel

If you live in an area where large logs are plentiful, or when a mature tree has been cut down on your property, you can use 6-inch lengths of sawn wood, set on end, to make a practical, appealing footpath. Hold off wood rot by soaking the sawn sections in chemical preservative for at least 24 hours.

Laying a log pathway

Excavate the pathway area to a depth of 8 inches, then spread a 2-inch deep layer of gravel and sand mix across the bottom. Level the bed with a straight board and compact it with a lawn roller or plate compactor.

Place the logs on end on the bed, arranging them to create a pleasing combination of shapes and sizes **(1)**. Work the logs down into the sand until they stand firmly and evenly. Then fill the spaces by pouring more sand and gravel between them **(2)**. Finally, brush filler across the pathway in all directions until the gaps between logs are flush with the surrounding surfaces **(3)**. If any of the logs stand too high, tap them down with a heavy hammer.

Cobblestones and gravel are used more for their decorative qualities than as practical paving. Cobbles, in particular, are uncomfortable to walk on and, although a firmly consolidated area of gravel is fine for vehicles, walking on a gravel footpath can be annoying. Both materials come into their own, however, when used as a contrast for areas of flat paving slabs or bricks and to set off plantings of any type.

Laying decorative cobbles

Cobbles can be laid loose, usually with larger rocks and plants. However, they are often set in mortar or concrete to create more formal areas.

Compact a subbase of gravel and cover it with a leveled layer of dry concrete mix, about 2 inches deep. Press the cobbles into the dry mix, packing them tightly together and leaving them projecting well above the concrete mix. Use a heavy board to tamp the area level, then lightly sprinkle the whole area with water. This will begin the concrete-hardening process and also clean the surfaces of the cobbles.

Laying gravel

If an area of gravel is going to be used as a pathway or for vehicles, construct retaining edges of brick, concrete pavers, or pressure-treated boards. This will stop the gravel from being spread outside the planned area.

To construct a gravel drive, the subbase and the gravel itself must be compacted and leveled to prevent cars from skidding and churning up the material. Lay a 6-inch bed of compacted bank-run gravel, topped with 2 inches of very coarse gravel mixed with sand. Roll it flat, then rake a 1-inch layer of fine pea gravel across the surface and roll it down.

• **Compacting gravel**
A lightweight garden roller is fine for compacting soil or sand, but use one weighing at least 200 pounds when you want to compact gravel. You can also rent a vibrating plate compactor to do the job.

Press cobbles into dry concrete mix

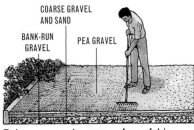

COARSE GRAVEL AND SAND
BANK-RUN GRAVEL
PEA GRAVEL

Rake pea gravel across surface of drive

1 Arrange logs on end

2 Shovel sand and gravel mix between logs

3 Brush filler mix into joints

Making a gravel garden
To lay an area of gravel for plantings, simply excavate the soil to accept a bed of fine gravel about 1 inch deep. Either set the gravel 3/4 inch below the level of the lawn or edge the gravel garden with bricks or flat stones. Scrape away a small area of gravel to allow for planting, then sprinkle the gravel back again to cover the soil right up to the plant.

Resurfacing with macadam

Stone chips

Dealing with weeds
Treat surface with weed killer two days before applying cold-cure macadam.

- **Treating surfaces for heavy wear**
Vehicle tires often cause excessive wear at entrances to driveways and on any curves. Treat the worn areas with a 3/4-inch rolled layer of cold-cure macadam. Apply a dressing of stone chips if you want.

- **Double dressing**
If the surface you are dressing is in a very poor condition or is very loose, apply a first coat of bitumen emulsion. Cover with stone chips and roll thoroughly. Two days later, sweep away any loose chips and apply a second coat of emulsion.

You can dress up an old macadam path or driveway, or any sound but unsightly paved area, by resurfacing with cold-cure macadam. It's a durable surface and is ready to use directly from the bag.

Choosing the materials
Cold-cure macadam is sold in 50-pound bags that cover about 10 square feet each at a thickness of about 1/2 inch. Both red and black versions are available. Some products are sold with a separate bag of decorative stone chips for embedding in the soft macadam as an alternative finish.

Macadam can be laid in almost any weather, but it is much easier to level and roll flat on a warm, dry day. If you must work in cold weather, store materials in a warm place the night before using them.

Preparing the surface
Pull up all weeds and grass growing between the old paving, then apply a strong weed killer to the surface two days before you lay the tarmac.

Sweep the area clean, and level potholes: Cut the sides vertical and remove dust and debris from the hole, then paint with bitumen emulsion supplied by the macadam manufacturer. Wait for the emulsion to turn black before filling the hole with 3/4-inch layers of macadam, compacting each layer until the surface is level.

Mask any surrounding walls and other objects. Then apply a tack coat of bitumen emulsion to the entire surface to make a firm bond between the new macadam and the old paving. Stir the emulsion with a stick before pouring it from the

Apply tack coat of bitumen emulsion

container. Then spread it thinly, using a stiff-bristled broom.

Try not to splash or leave puddles, especially at the foot of a slope. Let the tack coat set for about 20 minutes while you wash the broom in hot, soapy water.

Applying the macadam
Rake the macadam to make a layer about 1/4 inch thick **(1)**, and use a straight board to scrape the surface flat. Press down any lumps with your foot. Before the initial rolling, spread the contents of no more than three sacks. Keep the roller wet **(2)** to avoid picking up specks of macadam. Don't run the roller on grass or gravel, or you may roll bits into the macadam.

Spread and roll the macadam over the whole area, then compact it by rolling it thoroughly in several directions. Lightly scatter the stone chips, if you want, before the final rolling.

You can walk on the finished surface immediately, but avoid wearing high-heeled shoes. Don't drive on it for a day or two. And if you have to erect a ladder on the new surface, spread the load by placing a board under the feet.

1 Level macadam

2 Keep roller wet

As an alternative to macadam, you can completely resurface a walk or driveway with natural stone chips embedded in a bitumen emulsion. Stone chips, in a variety of colors, are available in 50-pound bags, one of which will cover about 3 square yards. Apply weed killer and fill any holes as explained for macadam (see left).

Bitumen emulsion sets by evaporation, but it won't be completely waterproof for approximately 12 hours after it has been laid. So check the weather forecast to avoid wet conditions. You can lay emulsion on a damp surface, but not when it's icy.

Applying the emulsion
Emulsion is sold in 10-, 50-, and 400-pound drums. A 10-pound drum will cover about 8 square yards, provided the surface is dense macadam or concrete. However, an open-textured surface will absorb much more emulsion. Pour the emulsion into a bucket to make it easier to use. Brush it out over the surface with a stiff broom. Follow the directions on the container and don't spread it too thin.

Spreading the chips
Having brushed out one bucket of emulsion, spread the stone chips evenly with a garden spade. Hold the spade horizontally just above the surface and gently shake the chips off the edge of the blade. Don't pile them on too thickly, just make sure the emulsion is covered completely.

Cover an area of about 6 square yards and then roll the chips to press them in. When the entire area is covered, roll it once more. If traces of bitumen show between the chips, mask them with a little sharp sand and roll again.

You can walk or drive on the dressed surface immediately. One week later, gently sweep away surplus chips. You can patch any bare areas that may have appeared by re-treating them with emulsion and chips.

Building garden steps

Designing landscaping for a sloping site offers plenty of possibilities for creating attractive outdoor features, such as multilevel patios, terraced planting beds, and undulating walkways. To be able to move from one level to another safely usually requires some steps.

Designing steps

If you have a large yard where the slope is very gradual, a series of steps with wide treads and low risers can make an impressive feature. If the slope is steep, you can avoid a staircase appearance by constructing a flight of steps composed of a few treads interposed with wide, flat landings, at which points the flight can change direction to add further interest and offer a different view of the yard. In fact, a shallow flight can be virtually a series of landings, perhaps circular in plan, sweeping up the slope in a curve.

For steps to be both comfortable and safe to use, the proportion of tread (the part you stand on) to riser (the vertical part of the step) is important. As a rough guide, construct steps so that the depth of the tread (from front to back) plus twice the height of the riser equals about 2 feet. For example, match 1-foot treads with 6-inch risers, 14-inch treads with 5-inch risers, and so on. Avoid making treads less than 1 foot deep, or risers higher than 7 inches.

Dealing with slippery steps

Steps can become dangerously slippery if algae is allowed to build up on the treads. Brush affected steps with a solution of 1 part household bleach to 4 parts water. After 48 hours, wash them with clean water and repeat the treatment if the fungal growth is heavy. You can also treat the steps with a fungicidal solution, but follow the manufacturer's instructions carefully.

Using concrete slabs

Concrete paving slabs in their various forms are ideal for making firm, flat treads for landscape steps. Construct the risers from concrete blocks or bricks, allowing the treads to overhang by 1 to 2 inches in order to cast shadow lines to define the edge of the steps.

So you can gauge the number of steps required, measure the difference in height from the top of the slope to the bottom. Next, mark the position of the risers with pegs, and roughly shape the steps in the soil **(1)**.

Either lay concrete slabs, embedded in sand, flush with the ground at the foot of the slope, or dig a trench for a gravel subbase and 4 to 6 inches of concrete to support the first riser **(2)**. When the concrete has set, construct the riser from two courses of mortared bricks, checking the alignment with a level **(3)**. Fill behind the riser with compacted gravel until it is level, then lay the tread on a bed of mortar **(4)**. Using a level as a guide, tap down the tread until it slopes very slightly toward its front edge in order to shed rainwater and prevent ice forming in cold weather.

Measure from the front edge of the tread to mark the position of the next riser on the slabs **(5)**, then construct the next step in the same way. Set the final tread flush with the paved area or lawn at the top of the steps.

Landscaping each side It is usually possible to landscape the slope at each side of a flight of steps with grass or plantings to keep soil from washing down onto the steps. Another solution is to retain the soil with large stones, perhaps extending into a rock garden on one or both sides. Eventually, spreading plants will soften the hard-edge look of the paving, but you should cut back overhanging growth that threatens to mask the front edges of the treads and cause someone to stumble.

1 Cut shape of steps in soil

2 Dig footing for first riser

3 Build brick riser and level it

4 Lay tread on mortar

5 Mark position of next riser

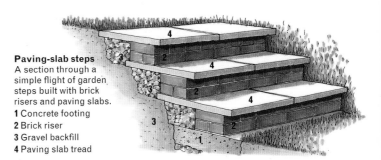

Paving-slab steps
A section through a simple flight of garden steps built with brick risers and paving slabs.
1 Concrete footing
2 Brick riser
3 Gravel backfill
4 Paving slab tread

Log and curved garden steps | Repairing concrete step

Concrete steps

Log steps

Curved steps

Paved circular landing

Building circular landings
To construct a circular landing (above), build the risers with bricks. When the mortar has set, fill the area of the landing with compacted gravel up to the top of the risers.

You can use sawn lengths of timber to build attractive steps that suit an informal landscape design. It's best to construct risers that are more or less the same height, otherwise someone may stumble. You can buy pressure-treated logs, machined with a flat surface on two faces. If you use untreated lumber, soak it in chemical preservative overnight before using it.

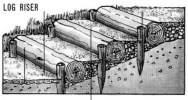

FINE GRAVEL   RETAINING STAKE
COARSE GRAVEL
LOG RISER
Log steps

Remove any turf and cut a regular slope in the bank, then compact the soil by treading it down. Sharpen 3-inch diameter stakes, cut from logs, and drive them into the ground, one at each end of a step **(1)**. Place a heavy log behind the stakes, bedding it down in the soil until it is level **(2),** and pack coarse gravel behind it to construct the tread of the step **(3)**. To finish the step, shovel a layer of fine gravel on top of the coarse gravel. Rake the gravel level with the top of the riser.

If large logs are not available, you can build a step from two or three smaller logs, holding them against the stakes with gravel as you construct the riser **(4)**. Finish by laying a gravel path at the top and bottom of the flight of steps.

Making curved steps
To build a series of curved steps, choose materials that will make construction as easy as possible. One option is to use tapered concrete slabs for the treads, designing the circumference of the steps to suit the proportions of the slabs.

Or use bricks laid flat or on edge to build the risers. Set the bricks to radiate from the center of the curve

1 Drive stake at each end of step

2 Place log behind stakes

3 Fill behind log with coarse gravel

4 Make up riser with two smaller logs

and fill the slightly tapered joints with mortar. Use a length of string attached to a peg driven into the ground as an improvised compass to mark out the curve of each step.

After roughly shaping the soil, lay a concrete foundation for the bottom riser. Build risers and treads as you would for regular paving-slab steps (see page 57), using the string compass as a guide.

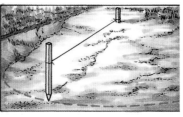
Mark edge with an improvised compass

Repairing concrete step

Pouring new steps in concrete requires such complicated formwork that the end result hardly justifies the effort involved. But if you already have a flight of concrete steps, you should keep them in good condition. Repair broken edges as soon as you can. Not only do they look bad but damaged steps can be unsafe.

Building up broken edges
Wearing safety goggles and gloves, chip away concrete around the damaged area and provide a good grip for fresh concrete. Cut a board to the height of the riser and prop it against the step with bricks **(1)**. Mix up a small batch of general-purpose concrete, adding a little PVA (polyvinyl acetate) bonding agent to help it adhere to the step. Dilute some bonding agent with water (3 parts water to 1 part bonding agent) and brush it onto the damaged area. When the surface becomes tacky, fill the hole with concrete mix flush with the edge of the board **(2)**. Finish the edge with an edging trowel, running it against the board **(3)**.

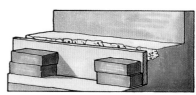
1 Prop board against riser

2 Fill front edge with concrete

3 Run edging trowel against board

Creating water gardens

There is nothing like running water to enliven a garden. Waterfalls and fountains have an almost mesmerizing fascination, and the sound of trickling water has a delightfully soothing effect. Even a small area of still water will support all manner of interesting pond life and plants—with the additional bonus of trees, rocks, and sky being reflected in its placid surface.

Pool liners

The current popularity of garden pools is in large part due to the availability of easily installed rigid and flexible pond liners, which make it possible to create a water garden with just a few days' work.

In the past it was necessary to line a pond with concrete. While it is true that concrete is a very versatile material, there is always the possibility of a leak developing through cracks caused by ground movement or the force of expanding ice. There are no such worries with flexible or rigid plastic liners .

Building forms for a concrete pond involves both labor and expense, and when the pond is finished it has to be left to season for about a month, during which time it needs to be emptied and refilled a number of times to ensure that the water will be safe for fish and plant life. In contrast, you can introduce plants into a pool lined with plastic or rubber as soon as the water is warm, which takes no more than a few days.

Choosing a pond liner

The advantages of manufactured pond liners over concrete are fairly obvious, but there are a number of options to choose from, depending on the size and shape of the pond you wish to create and how much you are planning to spend.

Rigid plastic liners Regular visitors to garden centers will be familiar with the range of preformed plastic pond liners. A rigid liner is in effect a one-piece pond—including planting shelves and, in some cases, recessed troughs to accommodate marsh or bog gardens.

The best pond liners are those made from rigid fiberglass, which is very strong and is also resistant to damage from frost or ice. Almost as good, and more economical, are liners made from vacuum-formed plastic. Provided they are handled with care and installed correctly, rigid plastic pond liners are practically leakproof. A very substantial water garden can be created with a carefully selected series of pond liners linked together by watercourses.

Flexible liners For complete freedom of design, choose a flexible sheet liner that will hug the contours of any shape and size pond. Flexible plastic pond liners range from inexpensive polyvinyl acetate and polyethylene sheets to better-quality low-density polyethylene and nylon-reinforced PVC. Plastic liners, especially those reinforced with nylon, are guaranteed for many years of normal use—but if you want your pond to last for 20 years or more, choose a thicker membrane made from synthetic butyl rubber. Black and stone-colored butyl liners are made in a wide range of stock sizes, up to 22 x 35 feet, and larger liners can be available as special orders.

Pond under construction
This ambitious project utilizes a flexible liner in the construction of a water garden.

Rigid pond liner
Rigid liners are molded from plastic.

Flexible liner
High-quality flexible pond liners are made from butyl rubber.

POND DIMENSIONS	
Length	9 ft. 9 in.
Width	6 ft. 6 in.
Depth	1 ft. 6i n.
SIZE OF LINER	
Length	9 ft. 9 in. + 3 ft. = 12 ft. 9 in.
Width	6 ft. 6 in. + 3 ft. = 9 ft. 6 in.

Ordering a flexible liner
Use a simple formula to calculate the size liner you will need. Disregard any complicated shapes, planting shelves, and so on. Simply take the overall length and width of the pond and add twice the maximum depth to each dimension to arrive at the size of the liner. If possible, adapt your design to fall within the nearest stock liner size.

Constructing a pond

A pond must be sited correctly if it is to have any chance of maturing into an attractive, clear stretch of water. Don't place a pond under deciduous trees: Falling leaves will pollute the water as they decay, causing fish to become ill or die. Some trees are especially poisonous.

Site and design considerations

Sunlight Although sunlight promotes the growth of algae, which cause ponds to turn a pea-green color, it is also necessary to encourage the growth of other water plants. An abundance of oxygenating plants will compete with the algae for mineral salts and, aided by the shade that is cast by floating and marginal plants, will help to keep the pond clear.

Water volume The pond's dimensions are important in creating harmony between plants and fish. It is difficult to maintain the right conditions for clear water in a pond that is less than 40 square feet in surface area. But the volume of water is even more vital. A pond up to about 100 square feet in area needs 18 inches depth. As the area increases, you will have to dig deeper, to 2 feet or more, although it's hardly ever necessary to dig deeper than 2½ feet.

Design The profile of the pond must be designed to fulfill certain requirements. To grow marginal plants, you will need a shelf 9 inches wide around the edge of the pond, 9 inches below the surface of the water. This will take a standard 6-inch planting crate, with ample water above, and you can always raise the crate on bricks if necessary. The sides of the pond should slope at about 20 degrees to prevent the collapse of soil during construction and to allow the liner to stretch without creating too many creases. It will also allow a sheet of ice to float upward without damaging the liner. Judge the angle by measuring 3 inches in for every 9 inches of depth. If the soil is very sandy, increase the angle of slope slightly for extra stability.

- **Accommodating a sloping site**
  On a sloping site, build up the low side with soil, planting grass up to the paving surround. Either cut back the higher side and build a low retaining wall or embed stones in the soil to create a rock garden.

- **Pool shapes**
  Although there's a huge variety of rigid plastic liners available, you are limited to the shapes selected by the manufacturers. There are no such limitations if you use a flexible liner, though curved shapes take up the slack better than straight-sided pools do.

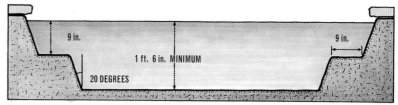
Important dimensions for a garden pond

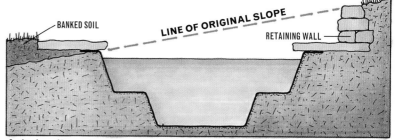
A sloping site

Installing a rigid liner

Stand a rigid pond liner in position and prop it up with cardboard boxes to check its orientation and to mark its outline on the ground.

Use a level to plot key points on the ground **(1)** and mark them with small pegs. You will need to dig outside this line, so absolute accuracy is not required.

Excavate the pond, then lay a straightedge across the top and measure its depth **(2)**, including shelves. Keep the excavation as close as possible to the liner's shape, but extend it by 6 inches on all sides. Compact the base and cover it with a 1-inch layer of sand.

Lower the liner and push it down firmly into the sand. Check that the pool is level **(3)** and wedge it temporarily with wooden boards until it is backfilled.

Start to fill the liner with water from a hose and, at the same time, pour soil or sand behind the liner **(4)**. Reach into the excavation and pack soil under the marginal shelves with your hands.

When the liner is firmly bedded, finish the edge with stones as shown for a flexible liner (on the facing page) or plant grass to cover the rim of the liner.

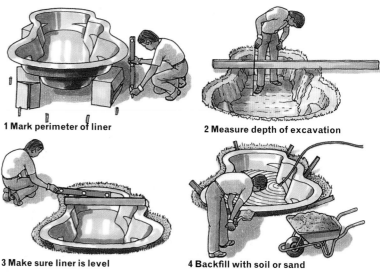
1 Mark perimeter of liner

2 Measure depth of excavation

3 Make sure liner is level

4 Backfill with soil or sand

Preventing ponds from overflowing

Every garden pond needs more water from time to time. But it's all too easy to forget to turn off the water and flood the garden. To keep your pond from overflowing, build a simple drain beneath its edging stones to allow excess water to escape.

Start by cutting corrugated-plastic sheet into two strips, about 6 inches wide and long enough to run under the edging stones. Pop-rivet the strips together to make a channel about 1 inch deep **(1)**.

Scrape earth and sand from beneath the liner to accommodate the channel **(2)**, then lay edging stones on top to hold it in place. Dig a small trench behind the channel and fill it with gravel, topped off with fine crushed stone up to the level of the edging.

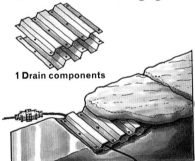

1 Drain components

2 Place drain beneath edging stones

Installing a flexible liner

Mark out the shape of the pond on the ground using a garden hose for the curved areas. Before you start excavating the soil, look down from an upstairs window (if possible) at the shape to make sure you are happy with the proportions of your pond.

Excavating the pond

Excavate the pond to the level of the planting shelf, then mark and dig out the deeper sections **(1)**. Remove any sharp stones and roots from the sides and bottom of the excavation.

The stones surrounding the pond need to be ¾ inch below the turf. Cut back the turf to allow for the stones and then, every 3 feet or so, drive wood pegs into the exposed surround. Level the tops of all the pegs, and use a straightedge **(2)** to check the level across the pond as well. Remove or pack soil around the pegs to bring the entire surround to a consistent level.

When the pond's surround is level, remove the pegs and, to cushion the liner, spread a ½- to 1-inch-thick layer of slightly damp sand over the base and sides of the excavation **(3)**. Pack the sand carefully into the soil.

Installing the liner

Drape the liner across the excavation with an even overlap all around. Hold it in place with bricks while you fill it with water from a hose **(4)**. Filling a large pond will take several hours, but check the liner regularly,

moving the bricks as it stretches. A few creases are inevitable, but you can avoid most of them if you keep the liner taut and press it into shape as the water rises.

When the level reaches 2 inches below the edge, turn off the water. Cut off the extra liner with scissors, leaving a 6-inch overlap all around **(5)**. Push long nails through the overlap into the soil, so the liner can't slip.

Laying the surround

Select flat stones that follow the shape of the pond, with a reasonably close fit between them. Let the stones project over the water by about 2 inches.

Wearing goggles, use a cold chisel and hammer to cut stones to fit any gaps. Lift the stones one or two at a time and bed them on two or three strategically placed mounds of mortar:1 part cement to 3 parts soft sand **(6)**.

Tap the stones level with a mallet and fill the joints with a trowel. Use an old paintbrush to smooth the joints flush. Don't drop mortar into the water or you will have to empty and refill the pond before introducing fish or plants.

1 Dig excavation as accurately as possible

2 Level edge using wood pegs

3 Line excavation with damp sand

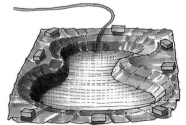

4 Stretch liner by filling pond

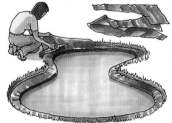

5 Cut flexible liner to fit

6 Lay edging stones to complete pond

Raised-edge ponds

Pumps and fountains

If you want a more formal pond, you can build a raised edge using bricks or concrete blocks. A surround about 18 inches high serves as a deterrent for small children while also providing comfortable seating. If you prefer a lower wall, say 9 inches high, create planting shelves at ground level, digging the pond deeper in the center. Place planting crates on blocks around the edge of a deep raised pond.

Building the edging
Pour 4- to 6-inch-deep concrete footings to support walls. Below is shown a typical cavity wall built to match the width of flat coping stones. The coping stones overhang the water's edge by 2 inches and the outer wall side by ½ to ¾ inch. To save money, you may prefer to use common bricks or plain concrete blocks for the inner side, while reserving costlier decorative bricks or blocks for the outer side of the wall.

A raised pond can be lined with a standard flexible liner, or you can order a prefabricated fitted liner to reduce the amount of creasing at the corners.

Trap the edge of the liner underneath the coping stones.

Raised-edge pond
A beautifully designed water feature, built from artificial stone. The small cascade is powered by a submersible pump.

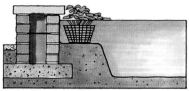

Partly excavated pond

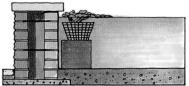

Fully raised pond built with a cavity wall

Alternative pond edging
Edging a pond with flat stones provides a safe and attractive footpath that is useful for tending water plants and fish, but often a more natural setting is desired, particularly for small pools in a rock garden. Incorporate a shelf around the pond for edging rocks. If you install them carefully, there is no need to mortar them in place. Add rocks behind the edging to cover the liner **(1)**.

In order to create a shallow, beach-like edging, slope the soil at a very shallow angle and lay large pebbles or flat rocks on the liner. You can merge them with a rock garden or let them form a natural waterline **(2)**.

To discourage neighborhood cats from poaching fish from your pond, create an edging of trailing plants. Without a firm foothold, cats won't try to reach into the water. Embed a strip of soft wire netting in the mortar below flat edging stones and cut the strip to overhang the water by about 6 inches as a support for the plants **(3)**. Once the plants are established, they will disguise the exposed edge of the pool liner.

1 Rock-edged pond

2 Pebble-strewn shelf

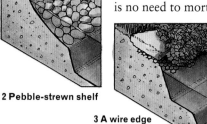

3 A wire edge supports plants

Submersible pumps for fountains and waterfalls are driven either by standard 120-volt power from the house service panel or by low voltage supplied through a transformer such as the ones used for low-voltage outdoor lighting (see page 70). The combination of 120-volt electricity and water can be fatal. If you don't have experience working with electricity, hire a licensed electrician to install the necessary equipment.

A low-voltage pump is safe and simple to install and wire. Place the pump in the water and run its cable under the edging stones to a transformer installed inside the house. Run the pump regularly, even in winter, to keep it in good working order. Clean the pump and its filter according to the manufacturer's instructions.

Place a submersible waterfall pump near the pond's edge so that you can reach it to disconnect the supply hose when you need to service the pump. Stand a fountain unit on a flat stone or bricks so the water jet is vertical.

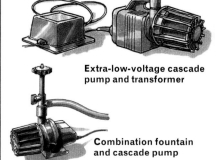

Extra-low-voltage cascade pump and transformer

Combination fountain and cascade pump

Solar-powered pumps and lights
Solar-powered fountain pumps and lights can be bought as complete kits, including a panel of solar cells.

The lighting units contain a battery that stores the electricity produced by the solar cells during the day, and releases it to the lamps during the night. The pumps are designed to operate continuously.

Building a rock garden and waterfall

Awaterfall running through a tastefully planted rock garden adds another dimension to a water garden. The technique for building a series of waterways is not as complicated as you might expect. While working on them, you can do much of the groundwork needed to create the rock garden. Providing running water is also an ideal way of filtering your pond.

You will be surprised at the amount of soil produced by excavating a pond. To avoid waste and the trouble of transporting it elsewhere, use it to create a pool-side rock garden. If you include a filter and a small reservoir on the higher ground, you can pump water from the main pond through the filter into the reservoir and have it return via a waterfall.

If you order them from a garden center, buying a large number of natural stones to give the impression of a real rocky outcrop can be extremely expensive. A cheaper way is to use hollow-cast reproduction rocks that after some weathering can look very realistic. Or you can order natural stones direct from a quarry and have them delivered or pick them up yourself, and buy or rent a heavy-duty wheelbarrow to make the work easier.

A rock garden and waterfall are best built as one project, but for the sake of clarity they are described separately here.

Avoiding back strain

Lifting stones
Keep your back straight when lifting heavy stones (right). Use a rope to lift and position large rocks.

Creating a waterfall

Rigid liner manufacturers make molded waterfall kits for embedding in rock gardens—you simply cover the edges with stones, soil, and trailing plants. You may prefer to create your own custom-made waterway, using pieces of flexible liner.

Installing the liner So that the waterfall can discharge directly into the main pond, form a small inlet at the side of the pond by extending a large flap of flexible liner **(1)**. Build shallow banks at each side of the inlet and line it with stones. Create a stepped waterway ascending in stages to the reservoir. Line the waterway with flexible liner, overlapping the ends on the face of each waterfall. Tuck the edge of each lower piece of liner under the edge of the piece above and hold the pieces in place with stones.

To retain water in small pools along the waterway, cut each step with a slope

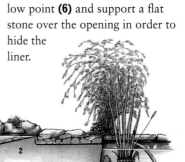

Constructing a rock garden

To create an illusion of rock layers, select and place stones carefully. Stones placed haphazardly tend to resemble a heap rather than a natural outcrop. Take care not to strain yourself when lifting rocks. Keep your feet together and use your leg muscles to do the work, keeping your back as straight as possible. To move a large rock, slip a rope around it (see left).

Lay large, flat rocks to form the garden's front edge, placing soil behind and between them to form

toward the rear **(2)** and place stones along the lip for the desired effect **(3)**. A flat stone will produce a sheet of water; a layer of pebbles will create rippling water.

As the construction work progresses, test the waterway by running water from a garden hose. It's difficult to adjust the angle of the stones once the waterway is done.

Bury the flexible hose from the pump in the rock garden—making sure there are no sharp bends, which would restrict the flow of water. Attach the hose to the filter tank at the top of the waterway **(4)**. Conceal the tank behind rocks where it can discharge filtered water into the reservoir.

A rigid plastic reservoir will have a lip molded in one edge, which allows water to escape down the waterway. If you use flexible liner to construct a reservoir **(5)**, you will need to shape the edge to form a low point **(6)** and support a flat stone over the opening in order to hide the liner.

a flat, level platform. Compact the soil to eliminate air pockets, which can damage plant roots.

Lay subsequent layers of rock behind the first ones, but not in a regular pattern. Place some to create steep embankments, others to form a gradual slope of wide steps. Brush soil off the rocks as the work progresses.

Pockets of soil for plantings will be formed naturally as you lay the stones, but plan larger areas of soil for specimen shrubs or dwarf trees.

Filter tanks
Pumps usually have built-in foam filters, but these are not sufficient to keep the water in a sizable pond clear and healthy enough for fish. It is preferable to install a plastic tank containing a combination of foam filters that will remove debris, plus a layer of biological filter medium to take out pollutants created by rotting vegetation.

Custom-made watercourse
This cross section shows a series of small waterfalls running from a reservoir to a pond.
1 Inlet
2 Sloped step
3 Edging stone
4 Hose run to filter tank
5 Reservoir
6 Reservoir outlet

Building a rock garden
A rock garden should have irregular steps along its front edge.

Conservatories

Ever since well-to-do people used them to raise exotic plants and as places for relaxation, conservatories have been desirable additions to our homes. Today, with double glazing and efficient heating, they are used not only as indoor gardens but as living and dining rooms, workrooms, studios, and sometimes kitchens.

Conservatories come in a range of standard sizes and styles. They are available as do-it-yourself kits but are usually professionally installed.

The materials used for constructing conservatories may include wood framing combined with low masonry walls, or they may be built primarily from aluminum or PVC components in a traditional or modern style.

The transparent sections of the roof may be constructed with glass panes or consist of double-wall or triple-wall polycarbonate sheets.

For security reasons and to conserve energy, double-glazed sealed units are now the most commonly used glazing for the windows and doors.

It is worth studying the range of available designs in order to choose a conservatory that suits the style of your house. For example, a decorative Victorian-style conservatory might be acceptable for a period house but would probably look out of place alongside a modern building. On the other hand, a simple modern conservatory can sometimes look perfectly at home with an older house. Overall proportions and the quality of the construction and the building materials are important factors to consider, too.

From the practical point of view, bear in mind that wood frames and panels need painting from time to time, and even

A well-constructed and insulated conservatory will add space and value to your home.

stained frames benefit from an occasional touchup with wood stain. Like PVC frames, factory-finished aluminum frames should require little, if any, maintenance.

Choosing the site

Some areas of the country may not require a building permit for a small conservatory or greenhouse addition, but most will. A quick trip to your local building department should answer any questions you may have.

Before committing to a design, check the manufacturer's specification in order to establish the size of the conservatory in relation to your site. Make sure there are no problems with drainage and with the proximity of trees or other features.

Apart from such practical concerns, which may include ensuring a means of access from the house, your choice of location should take into account the sun's direction. A conservatory built on a south-facing wall will benefit from sunlight all year and, as a result, would provide a cozy environment in the winter. However, in high summer the same conservatory is likely to become unpleasantly hot unless you provide efficient ventilation and shade.

A west-facing conservatory receives less direct sunlight, but could allow you to enjoy the setting sun during the late afternoon and evening. East-facing conservatories are ideal for an informal breakfast, with the possibility of early-morning sunshine. A north-facing site will receive little direct sunlight and to be comfortable will usually require heating for most of the winter. A corner site may provide you with a wide range of benefits for much of the day.

Heating and ventilation

Conservatories need efficient temperature controls if they are not to be too hot in summer or too cold in winter. The large expanse of glass is designed to absorb natural heat from the sun quickly, but it can just as quickly lose heat during cold weather.

Double glazing is essential to retain the heat gained from sunlight, particularly if a conservatory is to be used all year round. Ideally, low-emissivity glass should be installed, as it reflects the absorbed heat back into the room. However, during the winter months, when the sun's rays are weak and outside temperatures are low, it's necessary to provide internal heating. This is usually supplied by an extension to the house's central heating system or by individual space heaters.

During the summer, the heat can rise to uncomfortable levels. One way to overcome this is to install blinds for both the windows and the roof. Special heat-reflective blinds provide shade in the summer and reduce heat loss in the winter. Conservatory suppliers usually can provide blinds to meet your requirements. Another option is to stick special self-adhesive vinyl sheeting to the glazing. This reusable material can be applied to the inside or the outside and is held in place by static electricity only.

However effective your blinds may be, good ventilation is essential, not only to deflect heat in summer but also to reduce condensation in winter. Most conservatories have operable windows or vents to provide cross-ventilation. Roof ventilators are normally manually operated, but temperature-controlled automatic systems are also available.

Building conservatories

Although a conservatory is a fairly lightweight structure, it requires a strong base. Your existing patio, for example, probably won't do. A concrete base is the usual solution. But a special metal-frame platform, which requires less site preparation, is an alternative.

Conservatory suppliers will specify a typical base for their products. But because sites vary, you'll have to consult with your local building department to establish its requirements for foundations, perimeter drainage, and proper ventilation.

Types of concrete base
A typical base for a conservatory is a slab of concrete 4 to 6 inches thick, laid over well-compacted gravel that is a minimum of 4 inches thick. It should also have footings around the perimeter that conform with local building codes and suit the ground conditions. The base may be constructed as a monolithic concrete slab, which combines the footings (1). Or it can be built like a conventional foundation with concrete footings that support masonry walls, which surround the concrete slab (2).

The floor must incorporate a continuous vapor barrier underneath the slab to prevent water vapor and moisture from rising through the slab.

Constructing a base
To lay a standard conventional foundation, start by marking out the finished floor level with a chalkline on the house wall. Using form boards, lay out the area of the foundation, following closely the dimensions supplied by the conservatory maker. Use a plumb line to check whether the house wall is vertical. If it leans out, set the base dimensions from the plumb line, not the wall.

Footings should be 1 foot wide for a wall of single-brick construction, or 18 inches wide for a cavity wall with a 2-inch cavity. For most sites, footings must be at least 16 inches thick, starting at a depth required by your local building department. Dig the necessary trenches and pour inconcrete to the required level.

Let the concrete set, then excavate the area within the footings, allowing for the thickness of the floorcovering, concrete slab, insulation board (if required), and the compacted gravel base. Lay the perimeter wall up to at least 6 inches above ground level.

When the mortar has set, lay a bed of well-compacted gravel in the excavation and cover it with 2 inches of sand. Screed the sand until it is level. Then lay a polyethylene vapor barrier over the sand, with the edges of the sheet overlapping the inside surface of the walls.

You should seriously consider installing insulation board before you pour the slab. It will keep the floor warmer in the winter and cooler in the summer. Not all building codes require it, but it's well worth the money.

Complete the base (usually after you erect the frame) by pouring a concrete slab, followed, when fully dry, by the floorcovering.

Erecting the frame
The frame sills must be installed level and the modular frames mounted squarely. Following the manufacturer's instructions, erect the frame units. Any gaps at the junctions with the wall of the house should be filled with silicone caulk.

The roof-wall rafter should also be sealed and covered with a traditional aluminum flashing. If the house wall is brick, the step flashing should be tucked into mortar joints. If the house has wood siding, the flashing should be installed underneath the siding shingles or clapboards. The manufacturer's directions should explain how the flashing is joined to the conservatory roof framing.

Conservatory insulation
Some building codes require under-floor insulation only in rooms that are permanently open to the rest of the house. But it makes sense to include insulation in any case, as it will help conserve energy.

Foam insulation board, up to 2 inches thick, is installed as the floor is being laid. Insulation is normally placed under the concrete slab (1), but it can be placed just below the floor-covering (2). If the flooring is thin, like sheet vinyl, the insulation must go below the slab. If the flooring is solid wood, the insulation can go between furring strips nailed to the concrete slab.

1 Insulation under concrete slab

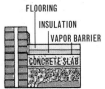

2 Insulation under flooring

Components of a conservatory
1 Concrete footings
2 Knee wall
3 Vapor barrier
4 Damp-proof course
5 Cavity insulation
6 Gravel
7 Concrete slab
8 Insulation board
9 Floor
10 Double-glazed wall units
11 Double-glazed roof units
12 Flashing

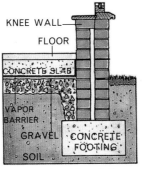

1 Monolithic slab foundation

2 Conventional foundation

Installing outdoor wiring

If you can do your own wiring inside your house, you can certainly do it outside too. The principles are the same. Because outdoor wiring is exposed to all kinds of weather, it must be impervious to water. It must also be resistant to the effects of extreme hot and cold temperatures. Knowing how to work with these materials is most of what you need to know to run electricity outdoors.

Working beyond the house
Outdoor wiring must be encased in conduit unless it is buried 30 inches deep. Fixtures and boxes, including receptacle and switch boxes, must be weathertight and rated for exterior use. Floodlights and their sockets must be rated for exterior use. As long as you meet these requirements, the improvements you make can be as varied as your outdoor needs.

Connecting to house circuits

You can bring indoor electricity outside with one of two exterior fittings, an LB fitting or a box extender:

90° LB fittings If you are starting with a new circuit in the breaker panel or tapping into an existing circuit with a junction box, the fitting you will use to get through the house wall will be an LB box. An LB allows you to come through an exterior wall and make a 90-degree turn along the wall. It is threaded on each end to accept conduit adapters or pipe nipples. Because it creates a 90-degree turn, its front can be removed so that you can help the wires make the turn. The coverplate for this opening fits over a rubber gasket, which makes the box watertight.

An LB is always installed between two pieces of conduit. In some cases, an LB might fit back-to-back with a junction box just inside the wall. Because no splices with plastic connectors are allowed inside smaller LBs, the conversion between cabled and individual

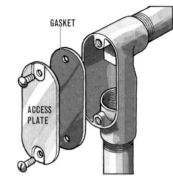

An LB allows you to wire at a 90° angle.

An LB and a junction box, back-to-back

made inside the junction box. Do not use an LB to exit a basement wall below ground. Use instead a junction mounted to the inside wall, then run conduit through the wall.

Extension boxes If you are tapping into an outside outlet or light fixture, you will not need an LB. Instead you can sandwich a weatherproof extension box between the receptacle or fixture and its outlet box.

To install an extension box, shut the power off at the service panel, remove the coverplate and receptacle or fixture, and pull the wires out of the box. Then screw the extension box to the outlet box mounted in the wall. Bring the conduit into the extension box and pull the conduit wires through the opening so that you can work on them comfortably. Connect all the same-colored wires to pigtails with plastic connectors. Attach the pigtails to the receptacle or fixture.

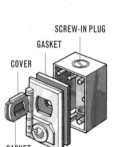

SCREW-IN PLUG
GASKET
COVER
GASKET

Outdoor receptacle box

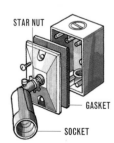

STAR NUT
GASKET
SOCKET

Outdoor floodlight box

GASKET
LEVEL
SWITCH

Standard switch with an external lever

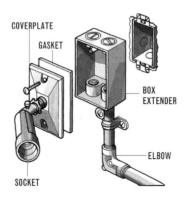

COVERPLATE
GASKET
BOX EXTENDER
ELBOW
SOCKET

Tapping an existing light or receptacle with a box extender

Connecting a new circuit
A box extender and metal conduit

Outdoor receptacles

Installing an outside receptacle mounted to your house is not that difficult. In most cases, tapping an existing circuit will work. Before you cut into any wall, however, shut the power off at the service panel.

Start by finding a receptacle on the inside near where you would like one on the outside. Then take careful measurements and mark the box location on the outside of your home. Hold a cut-in box against the siding and trace around it to mark the cut. To keep the corners neat, drill each with a ¼-inch bit. Drill completely through the siding and the sheathing. Then use a sabre saw to cut the box opening.

With the opening made, probe through it to find the existing box. If insulation is in the way, push it away from your work area. Then go back inside and remove the receptacle from the existing box and open a new knockout hole at the bottom of it. Push a short length of cable through the knockout opening until you think you've pushed enough to reach the new box. Go back outside and pull the cable out through the opening.

With the cable in place and the new box ready to install, pull the insulation back down. Insert the cable through a knockout opening and mount the box in the wall **(1)**. Install a GFCI receptacle in the box **(2)** and add a watertight cover box to keep rain out.

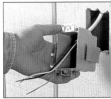

1 Slide cable into box; push box into hole.

2 Attach wires to GFCI receptacle and screw receptacle to box.

Isolated receptacles

To install an outdoor receptacle away from your house and nearer your yard or garden work, all you need is a few weathertight receptacle boxes, conduit, type UF cable, and the willingness to dig a trench between your house and the new receptacle locations.

Once you know where you plan to access the power from inside the house, mark this location on the outside of the foundation wall. Then drive a stake in the ground at this point and another where you want your first outdoor receptacle and stretch a string between the two. If you want more receptacles, run a string between each location.

Begin digging the trench, using a spade to cut the sod neatly about 4 inches deep and 12 inches across. Once cut, dig up the sod and pile it on one side of the trench. Continue digging until the trench is about 18 inches deep along its entire length. To protect the lawn, pile loose dirt on pieces of newspaper or a tarp placed on the opposite side of the trench from where you piled the sod.

With the ditch ready, run plastic conduit between the house and the receptacle locations. Cut the conduit with a hacksaw. At each receptacle location, sweep the conduit up out of the ground

Inserting the cable
Slide the cable through as you go.

with premolded bends called "factory elbows." Then use another bend to re-enter the ditch in the direction of the next receptacle. Factory elbows are connected with glue. You can install the electrical cable in the conduit after all the conduit is in place. But it's easier to slide the cable through the conduit before the fittings and pipe are glued.

To secure the conduit risers, or bends, slide a concrete block over each set of risers and pour concrete into the block cavities.

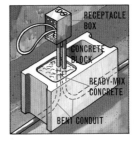

Supporting the conduit
Fill block cavity with concrete.

You don't need to wait for the concrete to set. Fill in the trench with the loose soil, tamp with your feet until firm, then replace the sod and give water it well.

With the conduit and supports in place and the wires ready, install a weathertight junction box on each set of two risers. Use plastic fittings that screw into the box and glue to the conduit risers. Of course, at the end of the run, you will have only one riser.

Finally, install the receptacles and weathertight coverplates and connect the conduit cable wires to the house circuit.

Other options Intalling landscape lights or a front-yard pole light does not differ that much from the procedures described here. The same techniques are used to carry power to outbuildings. Just remember that all wiring, except low-voltage systems, must be encased in conduit, and all fixtures must be weathertight.

Installing a GFCI
Every exterior receptacle or fixture must be protected from ground fault. When installing a new circuit, you might install a GFCI breaker, but when wiring only one box, use a GFCI receptacle. A GFCI receptacle senses any imbalance between the positive and neutral sides of the circuit. When an imbalance occurs, as it does with a short, the sensing mechanism immediately interrupts the flow of electricity. The only real difference between installing a GFCI and a standard receptacle is that a GFCI often has leads.

Working with conduit

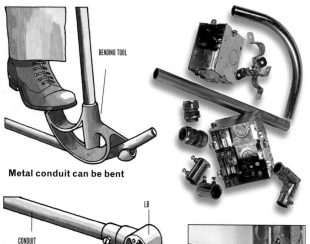

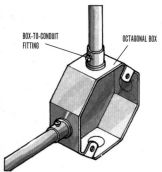

Not many residential electrical improvements will require the use of conduit, but some will, and you should know what is available and how to use it. Conduit is required any time individual wires are run in place of cabled wire. It is also required when a cable or wire is in danger of being cut, torn loose, or stepped on, that is, when it is in harm's way. There are several different types conduit.

Types of conduit

There are three basic types of conduit: galvanized metal, galvanized flexible metal, and plastic. All have at least two variations in wall thickness.

Metal conduit comes in 10-foot lengths and in three wall thicknesses. The heaviest is rigid metal. Rigid is usually hand-threaded and put together with threaded fittings. Because it is so heavy, you have to bury it only 6 inches deep in outdoor installations. The next heaviest metal conduit is known as "intermediate weight." It can be bent with a bending tool, so fewer fittings are needed. It can also be threaded for use with threaded fittings. The lightest weight metal conduit is called "thinwall." It is put together with threadless fittings. It can be bent and shaped to follow the contours of any wall, ceiling, or floor. Both intermediate and thinwall conduit must be buried at least 18 inches deep when used outdoors. Thinwall conduit is also prohibited for underground use in areas that have acidic soil compositions.

Flexible conduit resembles a hose more than a pipe. It is available in two thicknesses. It is very flexible and does a good job in protecting lead wires into appliances such as disposers, water heaters, and dishwashers. The NEC allows the heavier version to be buried, but many local ordinances disallow it for use underground. Flexible conduit is connected to appliances and outlet boxes with special clamp connectors.

As with plumbing pipes, plastic conduit is popular with homeowners. The reason is simple: Plastic conduit does not have to be shaped and can be glued together. (Electricians can shape plastic conduit with special benders that heat the pipe until it is malleable.) When you want a bend in a plastic pipe, all you do is buy a bend fitting and glue it in place. These fittings, called factory elbows, are available in 45-degree and 90-degree angles. Plastic pipe is especially handy when running wire underground and along support beams inside buildings. Because it is not as rigid as metal conduit, however, it should not be used out in the open where it cannot be secured to walls or other rigid supports. It must be buried 18 inches deep when used underground.

All conduit can be cut with a hacksaw or a sabre saw with a metal cutting blade installed. After each cut, be sure to trim the sharp burrs off the conduit before running any wire through.

Metal conduit can be bent

Attach conduit to box with connector

Metal conduit can be bent

LBs make fishing at right angles easy

CONDUIT
LB
COVER
CONNECTOR

Tee fittings join three pieces of conduit

THINWALL CONDUIT
OFFSET CONNECTOR
SWITCH BOX

Offsets keep conduit tight against walls

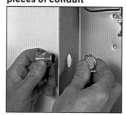

Connector joins conduit to panel

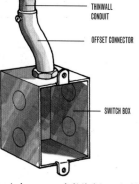

BOX-TO-CONDUIT FITTING
OCTAGONAL BOX

A junction box is used for splicing wires

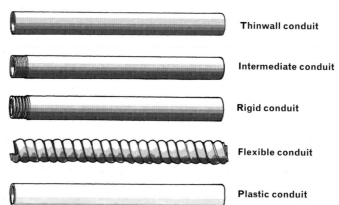

Thinwall conduit

Intermediate conduit

Rigid conduit

Flexible conduit

Plastic conduit

Installing a floodlight

There's no better way to extend the day than with a house- or garage-mounted floodlight. Aside from offering a measure of security and safety, a floodlight can also improve a wide range of outdoor activities, from backyard barbecues to nighttime dips in the pool, to after-dark driveway basketball games, and even to cooler-temperature, late-night gardening. If none of these ideas appeal to you, rest assured that most of them will appeal to the kids around the house. And to top it all off, floodlights are usually easy to install just about anywhere.

1 Find power source and knock hole in box

Access to power

In many cases the easiest access to power is through the garage. Unfinished garages make the wiring a breeze, especially if you don't mind having the switch in the garage. If this doesn't work for you, your next best choice is a ceiling fixture on a circuit that has room for another light.

Once you pick your circuit, shut off the power to it and remove the light fixture. Remove one of the knockouts on the side of the box and install 14/2 with ground cable into the box **(1)**. Attach it with a cable connector. Strip the sheathing off the cable and strip about ⅝ inch of insulation off each wire. Join the black cable wire to the black hot wire in the box with a wire connector. Do the same thing with the neutral cable wire and the neutral box wire. Join the cable ground wire to the other ground wires in the box. Replace the light fixture.

Run the cable to the switch box location and run the same-size cable from the switch location to the floodlight box location. Bore holes through framing members as needed **(2)**, and staple the cable in place at least every 4 feet.

Installing the fixture

The typical floodlight fixture consists of a metallic weathertight box, two adjustable lamp holders, a rubber weather gasket, and a coverplate. To keep water from entering the box through the cable opening, it's a good idea to install a plastic conduit nipple into the back opening on the box **(3)**.

Drill a hole through the side of the house and pull the switch cable through this hole. Then slide the floodlight box

2 Run cable through framing members to switch

over the cable and push the nipple on the back of the box into the hole. Screw the box to the side of the house.

To wire the fixture, join the cable ground wire, the fixture's grounding lead and a grounding pigtail with a wire connector Then attach the pigtail to the grounding screw at the back of the box.

Join the white neutral wire from the cable to one of the fixture leads with a wire connector. Then join the black cable wire to the other fixture lead with a wire connector. Attach the fixture securely to the box **(4)** and screw in the bulbs.

3 Thread plastic nipple to back of floodlight box

Connecting the switch

If you are working in an open garage you can use a standard switch box for this job. Just nail it to a stud about 48 inches from the floor. If the switch location is in a closed wall, cut a box hole where you want it and install a cut-in box **(5)**. A closed location will require fishing cable through the wall. Pick the most efficient route that does the least damage.

Feed the cable from the floodlight and from the power source into the box and strip the sheathing from both cables and about ½ inch of insulation from each wire. Join the ground wires from both cables to a grounding pigtail using a wire connector. Then attach the pigtail to the grounding screw at the back of the box.

Join both white wires in a wire connector. Then hook the black wire from the power source to one switch terminal and the other black wire going to the floodlight to the other switch terminal **(6)**. Screw the switch yoke to the box and install a coverplate. Turn the circuit power on and test the installation.

4 Attach fixture securely to the box

5 Push cut-in switch box into wall opening

6 Attach hot leads to switch

• **Floodlight options** Floodlights come in a variety of forms and are installed in a variety of ways. A quick trip to your local home center will reveal several design options. There are traditional fixtures, like the one above, and rectangular quartz fixtures. Some mount on the wall, others in the roof soffit, and still others have motion-activated switches. All have one thing in common: they are designed to be installed outdoors and so their components are weathertight.

Low-voltage lighting

Deck light

Well light

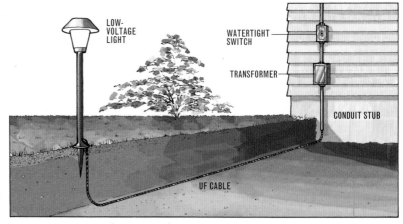

Mushroom light

Low-voltage wiring was once limited to doorbells and thermostats. Today, however, low-voltage lighting is being used in places unheard of a generation ago. The reason, of course, is that low-voltage systems give you more light for less money, and rising electric rates have made efficiency an issue. Low-voltage wiring is also safe; if you short circuit a low-voltage system, the shock you get will feel more like a tickle than the life-threatening bite of a 120-volt system. There are literally dozens of low-voltage systems available today, especially lighting systems. Pick whatever you want. None are hard to install.

Low-voltage kits

The best way to buy low-voltage components is in kit form. You won't necessarily save money, but you won't have to design your own system either. When you buy a kit, for example, the transformer size, the length and size of the wire and the number of allowable fixtures are all figured for you.

Contrary to popular opinion, low-voltage systems can start fires when overextended. Too many fixtures or too long a run can cause low-voltage wires to overheat. If you plan to design your own system, make sure you use a transformer with a built-in breaker.

Installing a transformer

In order to reduce your house current from 120 volts to 12 volts, a transformer is needed. There are several sizes of transformers to meet a variety of needs. Most transformers used in residential wiring are rated at 100 to 300 watts. The greater the rating, the more 100-foot branch circuits can be served. If a transformer is underrated, the lights it serves will not go on or the wire that serves them will overheat.

Transformers for indoor fixtures can be located in several places on or near their fixtures. In some fixtures, they can be part of an electronic circuit, similar to that of a stereo. But in many cases, you will fasten the transformer directly to a 120-volt metal outlet box. Just remove a knockout plug and attach the transformer to the box with a clamp. Then fasten the leads from the transformer to pigtail connections inside the box. The low-voltage UF wires can then be tied to the transformer's terminals.

A transformer designed to be used outdoors, however, must be sealed in its own weathertight box. You can buy transformers with on/off switches built in, or you can use a conventional switch between the outlet and the transformer. The transformer box must be connected to the outlet box with weathertight conduit. Then, from the transformer, low-voltage UF cable should be laid underground to each fixture. Low-voltage fixtures do not need to be grounded, and because they pose no physical threat, do not have to be buried deep or encased in conduit when installed outdoors. But it makes good sense to keep them out of harm's way, if for no other reason than you don't want to have to repair them after they're installed.

Low-voltage fixture connection

Low-voltage connections are made inside protective boxes on indoor lighting fixtures. In some cases, the low-voltage side of the fixture is wired and sealed at the factory. When you install these fixtures, you will only have to wire the 120-volt connection. The terminals on the low-voltage side of a transformer can remain exposed provided the transformer is not covered by drywall or otherwise concealed.

All outdoor connections must be made in weathertight boxes. This can be done the conventional way with binding screws or with special low-voltage connectors. These connectors use screw-and-clamp devices. The cable is placed in a slot and the clamp is screwed down over it. As the clamp tightens, it pierces the cable, making contact with the wires inside. In this case, you do not even have to cut the wire at the fixture. Both connections are code approved.

LOW-VOLTAGE LIGHT

WATERTIGHT SWITCH

TRANSFORMER

CONDUIT STUB

UF CABLE

Installing low-voltage outdoor lights

When it comes to electrical projects, installing low-voltage outdoor lighting is as easy as it gets. These kits are much less expensive to buy and operate than their 120-volt counterparts. For example, a six-head system uses about the same energy as a single 100-watt lightbulb. And the complicated weather protection and shock prevention measures required for outdoor 120-volt systems are almost entirely absent. Low-voltage wires don't even need to be buried deeply; a few inches are all that are necessary.

Shopping for lights

There are basically two categories of low-voltage lighting. At the low end are the familiar packaged kits, consisting of a transformer, cable, and six to eight plastic light heads. The head designs may vary and some kits come with light sensors that automatically turn on the lights, but most of the difference is only cosmetic. These kits are easy to install and are very durable.

Your other option is an à la carte mix of cast-aluminum fixtures. These lamps are considerably more expensive, but they usually look great, the lights are generally brighter, and you often have a bigger selection of styles.

Installing cable and fixtures

First determine the layout you want and mark the cable route. Do this from the transformer location to the last light. Then use a spade or flat-blade shovel to cut a slice into the ground about 5 inches deep. Push the shovel back and forth to create a V-shaped trench. Lay the cable into the trench, and wherever it sticks up, push it down with a wooden stick. There's really no depth requirement for 12-volt cable.

But a couple of inches deep offers the cable some protection and keeps it from being a tripping hazard.

The light fixtures come in different styles. The ones shown here are very common. Each consists of a stake, a riser pipe, and a lamp head. Each lamp head has a lead cable that passes through the riser and is fitted with a cable-piercing connector.

To install the fixture, drive the stake into the ground a couple of inches away from the cable. Make sure the stake is plumb, otherwise the lights, especially if they're lined up in a row, will look sloppy. Then slide the lamp head onto the riser tube and join the two with the set screw on the riser. Take this assembly and attach it to the stake, again by tightening a set screw.

Drive stake into ground

Connect lamp head to riser

Wiring the transformer

The transformer needs to be installed next to an outdoor receptacle. In most cases, all you have to do is screw the transformer box to the house wall and plug it into the receptacle. But systems do vary, so follow the instructions that came with your unit.

Next, bring the low-voltage cable up to the bottom of the transformer box and cut it to length. Split the last 2 inches of cable in two and strip about ½ inch of insulation off each wire. Crimp a ring connector (usually provided with the kit) onto the end of each wire. Then hook these connectors onto the transformer terminals. Install the transformer cover.

Attach ring connectors to ends of cable wires

Attach cable-wire connectors to transformer

Wiring fixtures

To make the fixture and cable connections, begin by checking that the cable lead from the fixture rests in its slot at the base of the riser. Then expose several inches of buried cable and lay it across the connector fitting on the end of the cable lead. Thread the fitting cap onto the fitting. As the cap is turned down, it pushes the cable into two sharp prongs that pierce the cable and the contact wires.

Make sure lead cable fits in riser slot

Lay cable in connector and tighten cap

Preventing wet rot

Rot can occur in unprotected lumber inside your house and in buildings and fences outside that are subject to moisture or high levels of water vapor. Damp conditions allow fungal spores to develop and multiply, until eventually the piece of lumber is destroyed. Severe fungal attack can cause serious damage throughout a structure and requires immediate attention. The two most common types are wet rot and dry rot.

Wet rot only occurs in lumber with a high moisture content. Unlike dry rot, which attacks wood with a much lower moisture content and occurs mainly in badly ventilated and confined indoor spaces, wet rot usually thrives outdoors.

Wood preservatives

There are many different chemical preservatives on the market, designed for specific uses outside and inside the house. Be sure you choose the correct one for the job at hand.

Liquid preservatives

For treatment of existing indoor and outdoor wood, choose a liquid preservative that you can apply with a brush. Although all wood preservatives are toxic, if you follow the manufacturer's instructions for proper use, they can be used safely.

Common preservatives are zinc and copper napthenate, and trubutylin oxide (TBTO). Traditional creosote and pentachlorophenol (penta) are no longer sold for consumer use. These chemicals are carcinogens and are highly toxic.

Liquid preservatives are sold in hardware stores, lumber yards and home centers. Some are also sold in paint stores. When buying preservatives make sure you get a preservative, not a water repellent. Preservatives carry antifungal chemicals that penetrate the wood. Repellents are exterior coatings that simply protect the outside of the wood against water damage. Some preservatives are paintable, others are not. And some come with stains incorporated into their formulation to color the wood.

Pressure-treated lumber

Pressure-treated lumber is the best choice for any new outdoor construction where the wood will come in contact with the ground or concrete. Decks and fences are the two most common examples.

Usually this lumber is rated for two different applications: ground contact and above-ground use. Inhaling the treatment chemicals can be harmful. So wear a dust mask when sawing and don't burn scraps.

Preserving lumber

Any lumber that's used outside should be treated with wood preservative. Brush or spray at least two coats on all boards, paying particular attention to joints and end grain.

Immersing lumber Lumber that will be in contact with the ground, especially fenceposts, needs to be treated with preservative. Either buy treated lumber, or do the treating yourself. Fenceposts can be coated on the outside by simply brushing on preservative. But the end of the post that will go in the ground should be immersed in a bucket of perservative to protect the end grain. Keep each post immersed for at least 10 minutes.

You'll get the best results, however, if you totally immerse the posts in a preservative bath. To do

Preservative bath

this, fabricate a tub by stacking up loose bricks for the walls and lining the depression with a thick sheet of polyethylene. Fill the trough with preservative and immerse the posts, holding them down with bricks to prevent them from floating. Leave them in the preservative overnight.

Treating wet rot

Once you have eliminated the cause of the moisture, cut off and replace any damaged wood. Then paint the repaired areas and surrounding woodwork with three heavy coats of fungicidal wood preservative. Brush the liquid into all the joints and end grain. Then apply a wood hardener to reinforce the damaged wood and fill any voids with epoxy wood filler. Finish up by priming and painting.

Safety with preservatives
All preservatives are flammable—so don't smoke while you are using them, and extinguish any open flames. Wear protective gloves and goggles when applying preservatives. And wear a face mask respirator when using them indoors. Provide good ventilation while working, and don't sleep in a freshly treated room for 48 hours to allow time for the fumes to dissipate completely. Immediately wash off any preservative from your skin. If some splashes in your eyes, flush them with water immediately and get medical help right away.

Clear   Wood Colored   Green

Building codes and permits

Building codes

Building codes are comprehensive guidelines intended to set standards for construction practices and material specifications. Their purpose is to ensure the adequate structural and mechanical performance, fire safety, and overall quality of buildings. They are also designed to address various health and environmental concerns related to how buildings are constructed. By setting minimum standards, building codes also limit unfair competitive practices between builders and between contractors.

Building codes address nearly every detail of building construction, from the acceptable recipes for concrete used in the foundation to the permissible fire rating of the roof finish material, and just about everything in between. Partly because codes attempt to be as comprehensive as possible, and also because they must address different concerns in different parts of the country, they are very detailed, complex, and lack uniformity from one region to another. A further complication is that many new building products become available each year that are not dealt with in the existing codes. Model codes, developed by four major organizations, are widely used for reference throughout the United States.

The Uniform Building Code, published by the International Conference of Building Officials, is very widely accepted. ICBO republishes the entire code every three years and comes out with revisions annually. A short form of the Uniform Building Code is available that covers buildings that are less than three stories high and have fewer than 6000 square feet of living space. This publication was designed for the convenience of most builders and remodelers.

The BOCA Basic Building Code, issued by the Building Officials and Code Administrators International is another widely used code. This code also comes in abridged form for residential construction.

A third model code, prepared by the American Insurance Association, and known as the National Building Code, serves as the basis for many codes that are adopted by local communities. It too is available in short form for matters relating only to home construction.

The Standard Building Code is published by the Southern Building Code Congress International. It addresses conditions and problems that are prevalent in the southern United States.

While it's likely that one of these model codes serves as the basis for the building code in your community, municipal and state governments frequently add standards and restrictions that are not in the model codes. It is your local building department that ultimately decides what is acceptable and what is not. Consult your building department for questions about any code issues. And keep in mind that building codes are primarily designed for the safety of the building's occupants and the general welfare of the community at large. It makes sense to follow all the practices outlined by the code in your area.

Building Codes

A building permit is generally required for new construction, remodeling projects that require structural changes or additions, and major demolition projects. In some areas, it's necessary to obtain a building permit for constructing an in-ground pool. In others, you even need a permit to erect scaffolding for painting your house.

To get a building permit, you must file an application (provided by your local building department) that answers questions about the proposed site and the project you are planning. You also have to file a complete set of drawings for the entire project along with detailed specifications for all the mechanical systems. A complete set normally includes a site plan, foundation plan, a plan for each floor of the house, section views of the house framing from the ridge to the foundation, elevation drawings of all four sides of the house, and drawings for all the mechanical systems. Permit fees are usually based on some percentage of the construction costs, or the numbers of trips that the inspector is likely to make to the job site, or both.

At the time you apply for a building permit, ask about other permits that may be required. For example, you may need to apply to the local health department for projects that have an impact on sewage facilities or water supply systems. It's important to arrange inspections in a timely fashion, since each ensuing stage cannot proceed until the previous work has been inspected and approved.

Anyone can file for a building permit, but if you've hired an architect or builder to handle the construction management for you, they should file for all necessary permits.

Building codes and permits

Type of work	Permit required		Zoning approval required	
Interior and exterior painting and minor repairs	NO	Permit may be required to erect scaffolding	NO	Unless in historic district
Replacing windows and doors	NO		NO	Unless in historic district
Electrical work	YES	Must be inspected	NO	Some outdoor lighting may be subject to approval
Plumbing	YES		NO	Work involving water supply or sewage system may require health department approval
Heating	NO		NO	
Constructing patios and decks, installing a hot tub	NO		NO	
Structural alterations	YES		NO	Unless house is in an historic district
Attic conversion	NO / YES	No, if work is minor like adding a simple bedroom. Yes, if major structural work is done and if plumbing and major electrical modifications are called for.	NO	Unless work impacts exterior of house in historic district
Building a fence or garden wall	NO		YES	In cases where a fence or wall is adjacent to public road, there may be height restrictions
Planting a hedge	NO	Unless it obscures the view of traffic at a junction, or access to a main road.	NO	
Path or sidewalk	NO	Unless it will be used by the public.	NO	Unless in historic district
Clearing land	NO		YES	
Installing a satellite-TV dish	NO		NO	
Constructing a small outbuilding	YES	Local codes usually have size restrictions. Anything smaller doesn't need a permit.	NO	Unless in historic district
Porch addition	YES	Local codes sometimes have size limits. Under the limit doesn't require permit.	NO	Unless in historic district
Greenhouse or sunspace	YES		NO	Unless in historic district
Building a garage	YES		YES	If used for a commercial vehicle or located close to property line
Driveway paving	NO		YES	At point where it meets the road
House addition	YES		NO	Unless house is in historic district or addition will be close to property line
Demolition	YES	If major work is done that involves any structural elements	NO	Unless house is in historic district
Converting single-family house into apartments	YES		YES	
Converting residential building to commercial use	YES		YES	

CHART
Building-code requirements and zoning regulations vary from town to town and frequently have county and state restrictions added to them. For this reason, it's impossible to state with certainty which home-improvement projects require official permission and which do not. This chart lists some of the most frequently undertaken projects and is meant to serve as a rough guide only. Taken as a whole, it suggests a certain logic for anticipating what type of approval may be needed. Whether or not official approval is required, all work should be carried out to the standards established in local codes.

Builder's tools

CROWBAR

A crowbar, or wrecking bar, is used for demolishing lumber framework. Force the flat tip between the components and use the leverage of the long shaft to pry them apart. Choose a crowbar that has a claw at one end for removing large nails.

Slater's ripper

To replace individual slates or wooden shingles you must cut their fixing nails without disturbing the pieces overlapping them, and for this you need a slater's ripper. Pass the long hooked blade up between the shingles, locate one of the hooks over the fixing nail, and pull down sharply to cut it.

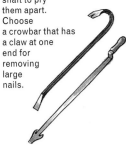

● **Essential tools**
Glass cutter
Putty knife
Cold chisel
Brick chisel
Spade
Shovel
Rake
Wheelbarrow
Cabinet screwdriver
Phillips-head
  screwdriver
Jack plane

GLAZIER'S TOOLS

Glass is such a hard and brittle material that it can only be worked with specialized tools.

Glass cutter

A glass cutter does not actually cut glass but merely scores a line in it. This is done by a tiny hardened-steel wheel or a chip of industrial diamond mounted in a penlike holder. The glass breaks along the scored line when pressure is applied to it.

Beam-compass cutter

A beam-compass cutter is for scoring circles on glass that enable you to either cut a round hole or create a circular pane. The cutting wheel is mounted at the end of an adjustable beam that turns on a central pivot that's attached to the glass by a suction cup.

Spear-point glass drill

A glass drill has a flat tungsten-steel tip shaped like a spearhead. The shape of the tip is designed to reduce friction that would otherwise crack the glass, but it does need lubricating with oil or water during drilling.

Hacking knife

A hacking knife is often a shop-made tool with a heavy steel blade for chipping old putty out of window rabbets in order to remove the glass. To use it, place the point between the putty and the frame, then tap the back of the blade with a hammer.

Putty knife

The blade of a putty knife is used for shaping and smoothing fresh putty when reglazing a window. You can choose between a chisel type with a thick, stiff blade, or a standard putty knife with a thin, flexible blade. Putty knives are also useful for removing paint and other light-duty scraping jobs.

CHISELS

As well as chisels for cutting and paring wood joints, you'll need some special ones when you are working on masonry.

Cold chisel

Cold chisels are made from solid-steel-hexagonal-section rod. They are primarily for cutting metal bars and chopping the heads off rivets, but a builder will use one for cutting a notch in brickwork or for chopping hardware embedded in brick.
  Slip a plastic safety sleeve over the chisel to protect your hand from a misplaced blow with a hammer.

Plugging chisel

A plugging chisel has a narrow, flat tip for cutting out old or eroded pointing. It's worth having when you have a large area of brickwork to repoint.

Brick chisel

The wide blade of a brick chisel is designed for cutting bricks and concrete blocks. It is also useful for other heavy chopping and prying jobs.

WORK GLOVES

Wear strong work gloves whenever you are carrying paving rubble, concrete blocks, or rough lumber. Ordinary gardening gloves are better than none, but they won't last very long on a building site. The best work gloves have leather palms and fingers, although you may prefer a pair with ventilated backs for comfort in hot weather.

DIGGING TOOLS

Much building work requires some kind of digging—for making footing trenches and holes for concrete pads, sinking rows of postholes, and so on. You probably have the basic tools in your garden shed; the others you can rent.

Pickax

Use a medium-weight pickax to break up heavily compacted soil—especially if it contains a lot of buried rubble.

Mattock

The wide blade of a mattock is ideal for breaking up heavy clay soil, and it's better than an ordinary pickax for ground that's riddled with tree roots.

Spade

Buy a good-quality spade for excavating soil and mixing concrete. One with a stainless-steel blade is best, but alloy steel lasts reasonably well. Choose a strong hardwood or reinforced fiberglass shaft with a D-shaped handle that's riveted with metal plates on its crosspiece. Make sure the hollow shaft socket and blade are forged in one piece. Although square spade blades seem to be more popular, many builders prefer a round-mouth spade with a long pole handle for digging deep holes and trenches.

Shovel

You can use a spade for mixing and placing concrete or mortar, but the raised edges of a shovel retain it better.

Garden rake

Use an ordinary garden rake for spreading gravel or leveling wet concrete. Be sure to wash your rake before concrete sets on it.

Posthole auger

Rent a posthole auger to dig narrow holes for fence- and gateposts. You drive it into the ground like a corkscrew, then pull out the plugs of earth.

Wheelbarrow

Most garden wheelbarrows are not strong enough for construction, which generally involves carting heavy loads of rubble and wet concrete. Unless the tubular underframe of the wheelbarrow is rigidly braced, the wheelbarrow's thin metal body will distort and may well spill its load as you are crossing rough ground.
  Check, too, that the axle is fastened securely—a cheap wheelbarrow can lose its wheel as you are tipping a load into place.

SCREWDRIVERS

Most people gradually acquire an assortment of screwdrivers over a period of time, as and when the need arises. Alternatively, buy a power screwdriver with a range of bits or buy screwdriver bits for your power drill.

Cabinet screwdriver

Buy at least one large flat-tip screwdriver. The fixed variety is quite adequate, but a pump-action one, which drives large screws very quickly, is useful when assembling large projects.

Phillips-head screwdriver

Choose the size and type of Phillips-head screwdriver to suit the work at hand. There is no "most-useful size," as each driver must fit a screw slot exactly.

PLANES

Furniture building may call for molding or grooving planes, but most household joinery needs only a light pass to remove saw marks and leave a fairly smooth finish.

Jack plane

A jack plane, which is a medium-size bench plane, is the most versatile general-purpose tool.

DECORATOR'S TOOL KIT

Most do-it-yourselfers collect a fairly extensive set of tools for decorating their houses or apartments. Although traditionalists will want to stick to time-tested tools and to materials of proven reliability, others may prefer to try recent innovations aimed at making the work easier and faster for the home decorator.

TOOLS FOR PREPARATION

Whether you're tiling, painting, or papering, make sure the surface to which the materials will be applied is sound and clean.

Straight scraper

Serrated scraper

Wallpaper and paint scrapers

The wide, stiff blade of a scraper is for removing softened paint or soaked wallpaper. The best scrapers have high-quality steel blades and riveted handles.

One with a blade 4 to 5 inches wide is best for stripping wallpaper, while a narrow one, no more than 1 inch wide, is better for

removing paint from window frames and doorframes.

A serrated scraper will score impervious wallcoverings so that water or stripping solution can penetrate faster, but take care not to damage the wall itself.

Vinyl gloves

Most people wear ordinary household "rubber" gloves as protection for their hands when washing down or preparing paintwork—but tough PVC work gloves are more durable and will protect your skin against many harmful chemicals.

Steam wallpaper stripper

To remove wallpaper quickly (especially thick wallcoverings), either buy or rent an electric steam-generating stripper.

All steam strippers work on similar principles—but follow any specific safety instructions that come with the machine.

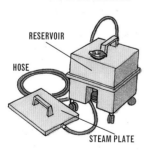

RESERVOIR

HOSE

STEAM PLATE

Using a steam stripper

Fill the stripper's reservoir with water and plug the tool into an outlet. Hold the steaming plate against the wallpaper until it is soft enough to be removed with a scraper. You will find that some wall-coverings take longer to soften than others.

Wallpaper scorer

Running a scorer across a wall punches minute perforations through the paper so that water or steam can penetrate faster. Some wallpaper scorers can be mounted on an extension handle.

Straight-sided shavehook

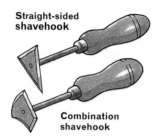

Combination shavehook

Shavehook

This is a special scraper for removing old paint and varnish. A straight-sided triangular shavehook is fine for scraping flat surfaces, but one with a combination blade can be used on concave and convex moldings too. Pull the shavehook toward you to remove the softened paint.

Heat gun

The gas blowtorch was once the professional's tool for softening old paint that required stripping, but the modern electric heat gun is much easier to use. It is as efficient as a blowtorch, but there's less risk of scorching woodwork. With most heat guns, you can adjust the temperature. Interchangeable nozzles are designed to concentrate the heated air or direct it away from windowpanes.

Drywall knife

A filling knife looks like a paint scraper but has a flexible blade for forcing filler into cracks in wood or plaster. Areas of damaged wall can be patched with large versions of this tool.

Wire brush

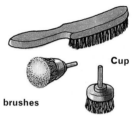

Cup brushes

Wire brushes

You can use a wire brush with steel-wire bristles to remove flaking paint and particles of rust from metalwork before repainting it. However, the job becomes easier if you use a rotary wire cup brush fitted into the chuck of an electric drill. Whatever method you use, wear goggles or safety glasses to protect your eyes.

Caulking guns

Caulk is used to seal joints between materials with different rates of expansion, which would eventually crack a rigid filler. You can buy caulk that you squeeze direct from a plastic tube, but it's more easily applied from a cartridge installed in a caulking gun.

Tack rag

A resin-impregnated cloth called a tack rag is ideal for picking up particles of dust and hard paint from a surface that's been prepared for painting. If you can't get a tack rag, use a lint-free cloth dampened with mineral spirits.

Dusting brush

A dusting brush has long soft bristles for clearing dust out of moldings and crevices just before painting. You can use an ordinary paintbrush, provided you keep it clean and dry.

SANDPAPER

Waterproof sandpaper is used for smoothing new paintwork or varnish before applying the final coat. It consists of silicon-carbide particles glued to a waterproof backing paper. Dip a piece in water and rub the paintwork until a slurry of paint and water forms. Wipe it off with a cloth before it dries; then rinse the paper clean and continue.

Alternatively, use a hard-foam block that's coated with silicon-carbide particles. These are somewhat easier to handle than a folded sheet of paper, which can tear or distort after a comparatively short period.

Woodworking tools

As well as the decorating tools described here, you will need a basic woodworking tool kit for repairing damaged floorboards or window frames and for such jobs as installing wall paneling or building shelves.

● **Essential tools**
Wallpaper scraper
Combination shavehook
Drywall knife
Heat gun
Wire brush

Decorator's tools

Masking tape
Low-tack self-adhesive tape is used to mask off wood trim or glass in order to keep an area free of paint when you are decorating adjacent surfaces.

Wide tape, up to 6 inches in width, is used to protect fitted carpets while you are painting baseboards.

Paint bucket
To carry paint to a work site, pour a little into a cheap, lightweight plastic paint bucket.

● **Essential tools**
Flat brushes
(½-inch, 1-inch, and 2-inch)
Wall brush (6-inch)

PAINTBRUSHES
Quality natural-bristle paintbrushes are made from black bristle or white ox hair.

Synthetic-bristle brushes are generally less expensive than natural bristle and are quite adequate for the home decorator.

Bristle types
Natural bristle is ideal for paintbrushes, since each hair tapers naturally and splits at the tip into even finer filaments that hold paint well. Bristle is also tough and resilient and meant for use with oil-based paint only.

Synthetic "bristle" (usually made of nylon or polyester) resembles real bristle, and a good-quality nylon or polyester brush will serve most painters as well as a bristle one.

Choosing a brush
The bristles, or filaments, of a good brush are densely packed. When you fan them with your fingers they should spring back into shape immediately. Flex the tip of the brush against your hand to see if any bristles work loose. Even a good brush will shed a few bristles at first, but never clumps of them. The ferrule should be fixed firmly to the handle.

½-inch   1-inch   2-inch

STORING PAINTBRUSHES
Before storing a clean paintbrush, fold paper over it and secure the paper to the ferrule with an elastic band.

Straight paintbrushes
The bristles or filaments are set in plastic and bound to the wooden or plastic handle with a pressed-metal ferrule. You will need several sizes, up to 3 inches, for painting, varnishing, and staining woodwork.

Cutting-in brush
The bristles of a cutting-in brush are cut at an angle so that you can paint windows right up into the corners and against the glass. Most painters keep a few sizes on hand.

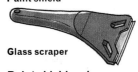

Paint shield

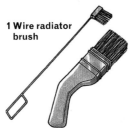

Glass scraper

Paint shield and scraper
There are various plastic and metal shields for protecting glass when you are painting windows. If the glass does get spattered, it can be cleaned with a razor scraper.

1 Wire radiator brush

2 Plastic radiator brush

Radiator brush
Unless you take a radiator off the wall for decorating, you will need a special brush to paint the back of it and the wall behind. There are two types of radiator brush. The one has a standard flat paintbrush head at right angles to a long wire handle **(1)**; the other is like an ordinary paintbrush but has an angled plastic handle **(2)**.

Wall brush
When applying latex paint by brush, use a straight 6-inch wall brush designed for the purpose.

CLEANING PAINTBRUSHES
● **Water-based paints**
As soon as you finish working, wash the filaments with warm soapy water, flexing them between your fingers to work the paint out of the roots. Then rinse the brush in clean water and shake out the excess. Smooth the bristles and slip an elastic band around their tips to hold the shape of the filling while it is drying.

● **Solvent-based paints**
If you're using solvent-based paints, you can suspend the brush overnight in solvent.

SPECIAL-EFFECT BRUSHES AND TOOLS
You will need to invest in a few specialized brushes and tools in order to paint your walls, ceilings, and woodwork with colorful textures. Most can be bought inexpensively from paint stores and home centers.

Dragging brush
This brush has extra-long flexible bristles that leave linear striations in wet glaze.

Stippling brush
This is a wide flat brush with short bristles that are dabbed against a glazed surface to apply or remove color.

Stencil brush
A stencil brush has short stiff bristles. The paint is stippled through a cut-ut template that defines the shape to be painted.

Wood grainers
Special brushes and paint applicators are used to create wood-grain effects with paints and glazes. The delicate bristles of a softener, for example, blur the outlines of graining, while steel, rubber, or plastic combs can be dragged through glaze to copy straight-grained wood. A heart grainer is used to create bold heartwood

Holding the shape of a brush
Squeeze out the solvent before you resume painting on the next day.

When you have finished painting, brush the excess paint onto newspaper, then soak the brush in a bowl of thinner overnight. Rinse the brush with clean thinner before storing it to remove all traces of paint.

● **Hardened paint**
If paint has hardened on a brush, soften it by soaking the bristles in brush cleaner. It will then become soft enough to wash out with hot water. If the old paint is very stubborn, dip the bristles in some paint stripper.

graining, and other effects are achieved using rolled-up or folded scraps of cloth.

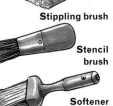

Dragging brush

Stippling brush

Stencil brush

Softener

Graining combs

Heart grainer

Glossary

A

Admixture
Any of various additives made for concrete and mortar mixes which provide or improve specific qualities such as appearance or weather resistance.

Aggregate
Particles of sand or stone mixed with cement and water to make concrete, or mortar, or added to paint for a textured finish.

Air-entrainment
An admixture that traps air in concrete to improve its weathering capabilities.

B

Ballast
A sand and gravel mix used as aggregate for making concrete.

Builder's sand
A fine, filtered sand used in cement or mortar mixes.

C

Cavity wall
A wall of two separate masonry skins with an air space between them.

Coping
Cutting a curved shape in wood. Also, a decorative molding covering a wall.

Course
A continuous layer of bricks, masonry, tiles, or other wallcovering.

D

Damp-proof course (DPC)
A layer of impervious material that prevents moisture from rising through the ground into the walls of a masonry building.

E

Efflorescence
A white, powdery deposit caused by soluble salts migrating to the surface of masonry.

Endgrain
The surface of wood exposed after cutting across the fibers.

Expanded clay
A cement aggregate.

F

Fall
A downward slope.

Featherboards
Overlapping planks that taper across their width, from a wide edge to a thin edge.

Fish tails
A metal wall tie with forked ends used to reinforce vertical joints in brickwork.

Flashing
A weatherproof junction between a roof and a wall or chimney, or between one roof and another.

Footing
A narrow concrete foundation for a wall.

Formwork
A frame which provides a mold for setting wet concrete, for floors, paths, and stairs.

Frog
The angled depression in one face of a type of brick.

Frost line
The boundary below which soil will not freeze.

G

GFCI
Ground fault circuit interrupter.

Glazier
A glassworker.

Grain
The general direction of wood fibers. Also, the patterns produced on the surface of lumber by cutting through the fibers.

H

Hardscaping
The paths, brickwork, patios, walls, and other built portions of a landscape design.

Hardwood
Timber cut from deciduous trees.

Heave
An upward swelling of the ground caused by freezing.

I

Insulation
Materials used to reduce the transmission of heat or sound. Also, nonconductive material surrounding electrical wires or connections to prevent the passage of electricity.

L

LB box
An electrical housing which allows you to connect electrical conduit at right angles.

Lead
A stepped section of brickwork built at each end of a wall to act as a guide to the intermediate coursing.

Level
To make perfectly horizontal or vertical. Also, an instrument, with a visible bubble of liquid, which measures the level quality of a structure.

M

Mattock
An axelike digging tool.

P

Pentachlorophenol
A substance used as a fungicide and preserver for wood.

Pier
A supporting column built at intervals into brick or block walls.

Plumb
To check the vertical aspect of a workpiece or structure for level. Also, a weighted line used to check the vertical.

Pointing
To form the mortar joints binding bricks together.

Polyethylene
A moisture-resistant, lightweight plastic.

Portland cement
A fine-grained aggregate of clay and limestone or similar substances.

Primer
The first coat of a paint system, serving to protect the workpiece and reduce absorption of subsequent coats.

R

Rebar
Steel reinforcing rod, used in concrete to add strength.

Riser
The vertical part of a step. Also, a pipe which supplies water, by pressure, to upward locations.

S

Screed
A thin layer of mortar applied to give a smooth surface to concrete or other mortar. Also, to smooth a concrete surface until it is flat.

Spalling
Flaking of the outer face of masonry caused by expanding moisture in icy conditions.

Squint corner
A pinched corner on bricks or blocks.

Stucco
A thin layer of cement-based mortar applied to walls to provide a protective or decorative finish. Also, to apply the mortar.

Subsidence
A sinking of the ground caused by the shrinkage of excessively dry soil.

T

Tamp
To pack down firmly with repeated blows.

TBTO
Tributyltin oxide, a fungicide used in liquid wood preservative to protect wood from weather and infestation.

Thinner
A solvent used to dilute paint or varnish.

Topcoat
The outer layer of a paint system.

Tread
The horizontal part of a step.

U

Undercoat
A layer or layers of paint used to obliterate the color of a primer and build a protective layer of paint before applying a topcoat.

V

Vapor barrier
A layer of impervious material which prevents the passage of moisture-laden air.

W

Wall tie
A usually metal piece used to reinforce joints in brickwork and masonry.

Index

Index